TAKE CHARGE
A Personal Guide
to Behavior
Modification

School of Divinity

Gardner-Webb University
School of Divinity

TAKE CHARGE
A Personal Guide to Behavior Modification

William H. Redd, Ph.D., and William Sleator

RANDOM HOUSE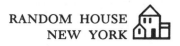
NEW YORK

Copyright © 1976 by William H. Redd and William W. Sleator

All rights reserved under International and Pan-American Copyright Conventions. Published in the United States by Random House, Inc., New York, and simultaneously in Canada by Random House of Canada Limited, Toronto.

Library of Congress Cataloging in Publication Data

Redd, William H

Take Charge: A Personal Guide to Behavior Modification

Includes index.
1. Behavior modification.   I. Sleator, William, joint author.   II. Title.
BF637.B4R4   153.8'5   76-27750
ISBN 0-394-40910-8

This book is not intended to serve as a self-help manual.

Manufactured in the United States of America
2 3 4 5 6 7 8 9

Grateful acknowledgment is made to the following for permission to reprint previously published material:

Journal of Applied Behavior Analysis: Excerpts from pages 160 and 163 of monograph # 2 entitled "Some Generalization and Follow-up Measures on Autistic Children in Behavior Therapy" by O.I. Lovaas, R. Koegel, R. Simmons and J.S. Long, Reprinted from Vol. 6, 1973. Copyright © 1973 by the Society for the Experimental Analysis of Behavior, Inc.

The Journal of Special Education: Excerpts from "The Contingent Use of Teacher Attention and Praise in Reducing Classroom Behavior Problems" by W.C. Becker, C.H. Madsen, C.R. Arnold and D.R. Thomas. Reprinted from pages 292, 294, 296 of Vol. 1, 1967.

Macmillan Publishing Co., Inc.: Excerpts from pages 64–66 of *Patterns of Psychopathology* by Melvin Zax and George Stricker. Copyright © 1963 by Macmillan Publishing Co., Inc.

Pergamon Press, Inc.: Excerpts from "Cognitive Change Methods" in *Helping People Change*, ed. by M.R. and A.P. Goldfried, pages 97–98.

Mr. Arpiar G. Saunders: For use of his letter addressed to Dr. P.J. Ciccone of the Medical Center for Federal Prisoners.

Acknowledgments

Esther Sleator, Lindley Redd, Rina Ullmann, Steven Stern, Donna Schmidt, Vicky Sleator, Sidney Bijou, Nancy Squires, Gordon Paul, Albert Porterfield, Norman Baxley, Linda Plotner, Sharon Rose, Stephanie Stolz, Arpiar Saunders, Marjorie Larner, Jane Schuman and Susan Bolotin

Contents

TAKE CHARGE
A Personal Guide to Behavior Modification

Applied Common Sense

It is the fourth time Brian K. has phoned Susan B. to ask her
for a date. She's perfectly pleasant, as usual. But also as usual,
she insists that she'll be "too tired" on that particular evening
and will not be able to see him. It is the last time Brian K.
phones Susan B.

Emmanuel G., a migrant worker, is picking lettuce. The
sun is hot, he is tired, but nevertheless he is picking lettuce very
fast. Emmanuel G. knows he is going to be paid not for how
long he works, but for how much lettuce he picks.

A group of political radicals kidnap an heiress. Several
months later she participates in a bank robbery. At her trial her
lawyer attempts to prove that she was coerced into committing
the crime, was not in control of her own actions and is therefore not guilty.

A twenty-seven-year-old accountant is learning to ski. His
instructor starts him on very short skis, which he can handle
easily while enjoying the thrill of swooping down a slope. As

he progresses he is given increasingly longer skis and soon is using long racing skis on difficult slopes, without ever having experienced the usual mishaps.

A rat in a laboratory frantically presses a little red lever at the rate of 200 times a minute in order to earn three pellets of food. A child touches a hot stove, burns his hand and does not touch the stove again. A pupil scores perfectly on a spelling test, the teacher puts a star beside her name on a chart, and that night the child goes home and studies the spelling words for the next day. A driver receives a ten-dollar ticket and becomes aware of "No Parking" signs. A shopper wanders into a store with a coupon giving him a discount on Cokes, and on his way to the soft-drink counter, located at the back of the store, happens to pick up a frozen cherry cheese cake and a box of pretzels. In a Las Vegas casino a woman on her hard-earned one-week vacation sits on an uncomfortable stool from 8 A.M. to 10 P.M., feeding nickels into a slot machine. And John M., noticing that his boss is red-eyed, disheveled and snapping at his secretary, decides to wait until next week to ask him for a raise.

What is going on here? Do these seemingly disparate situations have anything in common? Indeed they do. They are all examples of what a relatively new breed of psychologists refers to as the Law of Effect. In its simplest form, this almost absurdly obvious principle asserts that all living organisms—animals as well as people—will continue to do things that bring them rewards and will stop doing things that result in punishment. It's an idea that in itself is nothing new, of course. We're all aware of it; it's just a commonsense fact of life. What *is* new, however, is that psychologists have taken this everyday principle and analyzed it, systematized it, pursued endless manifestations of it—and have emerged with a revolutionary new perspective on human behavior. By-passing, for the most part, the traditional theories of inner states of mind, they concentrate primarily on outward behavior itself. These psychologists are now applying their extremely sophisticated reward-punishment systems, commonly known as behavior modification, to a wide variety of life situations. And they are getting amazing, and to many minds disturbing, results. Writing in the Washington *Post*, Nicholas Kittrie, author of *The Right to Be Different*, notes: "There is a behavior modification revolution upon us, which with its magnitude is not unlike the industrial revolution of 200 years ago . . . The new revolution aims at direct reform and control of man himself."[1]

And behavior modification certainly works. By means of a deceptively simple strategy of changing how the social environment responds to what people do, long-standing habits and patterns of behavior are radically altered. "Hopelessly" disturbed people who have been in strait jackets for years can now take care of themselves and lead more satisfying lives. Migraine sufferers are being taught how to reduce the intensity of their headaches; overweight people are learning how to get thin and then actually stay thin; insomniacs now have techniques that enable them to fall asleep quickly without using drugs; music teachers are capable of turning out orchestras of four hundred five-year-olds all playing the violin together, and mercifully, in tune. Indeed, it's reached the point where most of us would be hard put to avoid encountering behavior modification in some form or another. Teachers, prison guards, factory foremen and hospital nurses are discovering how effective its methods can be. In fact, its popularity is mushrooming to the point of faddishness. Television doctors Joe Gannon and Marcus Welby have recommended behavior modification, and within sixty minutes, their patients' problems have been resolved. There is even a group that calls itself the behavior mod squad. And its use is certainly not limited to professionals; during the past four years, at least thirty do-it-yourself manuals have been published for parents, as well as countless articles that Sunday newspapers and women's magazines run about behavior-modification programs for losing weight.

What is ominous about all this is how extraordinarily effective behavior modification is. There is no denying that it has the potential of delivering a most powerful weapon—the possibility of control—into the hands of the few. We all know that we influence, or in a sense control, one another. Clearly, the mother exerts great influence on the child, and the child influences her in return. But danger ensues when control is not balanced. Classic examples are the practice of slavery and the regimes of totalitarian governments. With behavior modification at its disposal, there is practically no limit to the control that one group of people could exert over another. In fact, the American Civil Liberties Union and the American Psychological Association are now investigating alleged abuses of behavior modification.

Many people argue that behavior modification must be stopped. And yet there are individuals with serious problems for whom these techniques offer the best hope. We are only beginning to explore the potential of behavior modification for *helping* the human race. The dilemma we face, therefore, is how to prevent misuse of the tool without denying people the right to effective treatment.

And the dilemma is an elusive one, far more complex than another central problem of our time, the nuclear menace. Atomic power is also a tool that has to be limited. But the limitations that we must impose upon atomic power are obvious: all we've got to do is make sure nobody ever presses the doomsday button—and we don't have to know how it actually works to realize that. In order to limit behavior modification intelligently, however, we *do* have to know how it works. Here is a tool of tremendous subtlety and variety that deals with our very essence—the human condition—and its still barely understood complexities. Its very existence, not to mention its application, sets up an endless series of moral and political, even philosophical questions that we all must be able to answer before deciding how it should be used. A clear and responsible consumer's guide is needed.

And beyond all that, every individual benefits from a familiarity with these principles of human behavior. Behavior theory provides us with a particularly apt and enlightening explanation of why we do what we do. And not only is it fascinating, it's practical. We should understand it because it is all around us. And once we do understand how it works, it cannot help but enable us to deal more effectively with many of the situations we face in life, with other people and with ourselves.

Behavioral Dynamics

The Law of Effect is a fact of life. All organisms are influenced by the consequences of their own behavior. It would be a strange world indeed if people persisted doing things that brought them personal pain and destruction. In fact, when people see someone violating this law they usually identify him as neurotic or even crazy, a danger to himself or society, and often institutionalize him. When you think about it, it's clear that the survival of mankind depends on our acting according to the Law of Effect. If our earliest ancestors had not eaten when they were hungry, protected themselves from wild beasts and from the cold, or made love when they felt like it, we would not be around today. In more scientific language, then, the Law of Effect states that the probability of a certain behavior being repeated is directly related to the consequences that behavior produces.

Behaviorists don't claim that they necessarily know or are always able to determine exactly what the rewards are in a particular situation. In practice they may be pretty sure why most of us engage in simple behavior like eating or sleeping, but when it comes to more complex behavior patterns they don't always know. For example, the behaviorists may not know why a particular child plays with his blocks. It could be because his mother gives him praise and attention whenever he plays with them, or because his mother scolds him for *not* playing quietly, or simply because he finds the blocks interesting. However, behaviorists are sure that the child plays with his blocks because such play yields positive consequences or removes negative ones. Such consequences are referred to as *reinforcers*—events that increase the likelihood that a certain behavior will be repeated. The present authors' writing behavior will probably be strengthened if our labor results in rave reviews, intellectual satisfaction and elimination of our debts; then we will surely be at it again. Now, if it is not reinforced but punished instead—if the book leads to ridicule and loss of savings—then our writing behavior will certainly diminish.

Of course, there are some things that are reinforcers for almost everyone, like food, water, sex—things that are vital to our survival. Love, attention and appreciation are also important reinforcers. But because of differences in personal tastes, preferences and "chemistry," the list of universal reinforcers is relatively short. A powerful reinforcer for one person may be of no value for another. A fourteen-year-old boy may find the ear-splitting sound of hard rock so pleasant that he works after school to buy records, whereas his forty-five-year-old father may find the sounds so aversive that he spends his hard-earned money on soundproofing. The son finds the music reinforcing, but the father deems it punishing. Likewise, Brahms and a glass of sherry may be a reinforcer for the father and a punishment for the son. To each his own.

Whether something functions as a reinforcer depends upon a vast number of factors, like how we feel, who is giving the reinforcer and how important the reinforcer is to us. But the most important factor is how and when reinforcers and punishments are experienced. If we receive a strong reinforcer every time we do a particular thing, it's highly likely that we'll continue doing it. If, however, we tire of the reinforcer because we've become satiated, the reinforcer will lose its value and our behavior will stop. A child might be anxious to do a favor for you if you'll give him a piece of gum for it, but he won't be so eager after he's filled his mouth and pockets with Dubble Bubble. The compliments of a new friend may flatter us and we may work hard to win his approval. If he dishes out compliments all the time and for everything we do, however, the compliments will soon begin to have little value and we'll eventually lose interest. This satiation phenomenon, though, does not apply to everything; for example, there aren't too many of us who ever tire of receiving financial rewards.

By studying the behavior of animals and people in laboratories and by carefully observing people going about their daily activities, psychologists have discovered a whole set of behavioral principles that have direct bearing on almost all of our actions, even the most complex. They express these principles in terms of the effects that different types of rewards and punishments have on behavior. To understand what they're talking about, we only have to look around us.

Most of us who have spent much time around young children have tried to settle a crying youngster. A mother is preparing lunch and her eighteen-month-old son is sitting on the kitchen floor screaming at the top of his lungs. She has already checked twice to see what's wrong. He has just finished his nap, he is dry and he is holding one of his favorite crackers. The room is comfortably warm and he can easily see his mother. But he continues to cry. Needless to say, the mother is frustrated; so in mild desperation she picks him up and holds him on her hip while she continues her chores. As soon as she lifts him up, he stops crying and becomes the picture of contentment.

Naturally, she is relieved that he is quiet and happy, but this has happened before and she has the sneaking suspicion that crying is his way of getting attention. Behaviorists would probably agree. It appears that the child's crying results in his being held. He obviously likes being close to his mother and he has learned an effective means of getting what he wants. According to behavior theory, each time the mother picks him up while he is crying the likelihood increases that in the future he'll cry when he wants her attention. The mother's actions are strengthening the child's behavior.

Of course, the mother should teach her son less annoying ways to get her attention by refraining from picking him up when he cries for that reason. But chances are that she'd find it very difficult to ignore his crying, even when she's sure that everything is all right. She hates hearing her baby cry and the sounds of his crying would punish *her* if she didn't pick him up. By the same token, she is rewarded by his quieting when she holds him. Both the mother's and the son's actions serve as powerful rewards and punishments, and since both are striving for the most positive state of affairs possible, the reactions of each affect the behavior of the other.

One very important factor influencing the effects of reinforcement is its timing. If, for example, we were in a situation in which reinforcers could only be given out at certain predictable points in time—say, once every half-hour—we'd most likely slow down and rest between the payoff times. Just think how a work crew relaxes and slacks off immediately after the foreman has left. If the payoff periods came more often and occurred at irregular and unannounced times, then we would work harder.

The most intriguing behavioral axiom is the seemingly nonsensical proposition that a reward given out more rarely can often have a far more powerful effect on behavior than a reward that comes every time the behavior occurs. Behavioral psychologists were certainly not the first to become aware of this rather paradoxical fact of life—owners of gambling casinos, factory foremen and grade-school teachers have been making use of it for years. Think of the lady and the slot machine. The owner of the casino wants to keep her sitting there feeding in nickels for as long as possible. She'd keep on sitting there for an eternity if she hit the jackpot every time, but then the casino owner would lose out. He could set the machine so that she'd win at first and then switch it so that he'd always win, but she'd soon stop playing if the payoffs suddenly slowed down and move on somewhere else. The casino owner knows this and has a very effective way of making sure she keeps playing: the machine is set so she gets some payoff every so often. Rewards —in this case jackpots—occur unpredictably, requiring a varying number of responses before a payoff. She continues to play "just one more time" because she doesn't know when she'll win, and the next pull might be the "lucky one." The machine is carefully set so that she'll win just often enough to keep her playing, yet infrequently enough for the owner to rack up a handsome profit. This canny method of timing the reward is called *variable-ratio reinforcement.*

There are lots of other less insidious examples of variable-ratio reinforcement. Teachers know that if they call on their students in alphabetical order, then those whose names begin with A will become less attentive once Bobby Brooks's and Betty Brown's turns have come up. And chances are that Tommy Adams won't start listening again until the teacher has finished with Tarry Zack and Mary Zoom. To minimize this kind of problem, good teachers begin by making their material stimulating enough so the students can't help listening. They also keep students on their toes by questioning them in an unpredictable order. If the students don't know when they might have the opportunity to give an answer, they'll be more likely to stay tuned in.

Many psychologists have spent their whole careers studying the relationship between behavior and the timing of reinforcement. To the amazement of many, these relationships are consistent for all individuals, holding even across species. At some point in almost every introductory psychology course, the professor demonstrates these laws of behavior with a white rat and a food dispenser. The animal is housed in a small box (sometimes called a Skinner box after the famous behavioral psychologist B. F. Skinner) with a small lever that delivers food when pressed. The experimenter sets the apparatus to deliver food according to some pattern—for example, after every five presses of the lever, the animal gets a pellet of food. Within a short period of time the rat is pressing the lever rapidly five times in a row and then grabbing his food. It almost looks as if our animal has learned to count. The pattern of reinforcement that produced this result is called *fixed-ratio reinforcement*. The pellets could also be delivered on a fixed-interval reinforcement pattern so that if the animal makes at least one press every x number of seconds, he'll get a food pellet. In this case the animal will slow down his rate of pressing after he receives a food pellet and then speed up only as the time for reinforcement approaches.

There is almost no end to the variety of patterns of reinforcement. If the schedule is especially complicated or there are long delays between presses and the delivery of reward, the animal will often develop ritualistic behavior unnecessary for getting the reinforcement. He might turn around three times or do a flip before he presses. If this behavior happens to get reinforced, the rat may come to "believe" that the flip is necessary, even though it doesn't do anything to produce reinforcement. In such cases, the professor identifies the rat's behavior as superstitious.

People develop superstitions too, and in much the same way. If a stroke of good fortune (reinforcement) occurs while we're wearing a particular article of clothing, we may easily come to believe that the purple shirt is our "good-luck shirt." Or if something really terrible happens just after we've walked past a certain house, we may well want to avoid that house in the future. Certainly people aren't as prone to superstition as rats, since people usually understand why they're being reinforced or punished, but sometimes people don't know. Because of accidental pairings of certain things we do, along with subsequent reinforcement or punishment, we believe that the actions will have some effect on what happens. Even though we may feel a bit silly about wearing that purple shirt we still do, just in case it might help.

Behavioral psychologists do not stop with simple behavior

—they also apply their principles to more complex and elaborate situations, such as international diplomacy. Oil-rich nations are now able to control our behavior because they hold valuable reinforcers, and in order to escape this control, we are trying to find other sources of oil—other sources of the valued reinforcer.

And let us not leave out romance, which is certainly not immune to similar interpretation. Psychologists have speculated that the stability of our close relationships with others lies also at the mercy of the Law of Effect. The ratio of reinforcement and punishment experienced in a relationship determines to a large extent the likelihood of the members staying together. When the costs, or punishing aspects, of a marriage or friendship start outweighing the benefits, then the partners begin looking elsewhere. If Bob yells at Margie more than he cuddles her, then she'll start looking for affection somewhere else, and if she finds it, she'll drop Bob—maybe. For there is also punishment involved in separation, and if Margie finds *that* particular punishment more severe than Bob's berating her, she may end up staying with him, after all. Some psychologists believe that we even select our friends and associates in terms of the reinforcement we get from their company. And it makes sense: certainly, we are satisfied if our personal life brings us joy and fulfillment, and we become unhappy when our relationships with people are painful, frustrating and unpleasant. According to behavioral psychology, a relationship is unsatisfying when it no longer provides reinforcement. To make a relationship better and more secure we must devise ways of increasing the amount of reinforcement it provides— which of course is easier said than done. And though this way of conceptualizing personal relationships may at first sound cold and calculated, it's really only a question of semantics. Essentially, behaviorists *are* talking about satisfaction, fulfillment and joy, but in their own scientific terminology—just the way a medical doctor might describe someone who is stuffed to the gills as suffering from a severe case of postprandial anorexia.

That brings us to unpleasant consequences—punishment. It comes in many forms and from many sources. If we break one of nature's laws, we often get hurt, and if we violate society's laws and are caught, we may get fined or imprisoned. There are also less obvious forms of punishment, such as sarcastic comments from others, failure and humiliation. And gasoline taxes, import tariffs and fines have the same effect. The negative side of the Law of Effect involves either loss of something good or the occurrence of something bad; in all cases the result is to discourage certain types of behavior and encourage others.

Many behaviorists feel that punishment is a bad thing; B. F. Skinner warns that it can have disastrous side effects and that it fosters subservience. Others claim that punishment just doesn't work. Textbooks and training manuals on behavior modification argue against using it. Perhaps it is because the idea of inflicting pain and suffering is repugnant that psychologists have tended, by and large, to oppose the use of punishment. In fact, the behaviorists' recommendations appear to be based on emotion and conjecture rather than on clear scientific evidence, for very little research within psychology has been directed toward the possible harmful effects of punishment.

It is not surprising that psychologists really know very little about how aversive consequences affect our behavior. But research with animals clearly shows that punishment does work. And what's more, it works fast. Animals learn very quickly to avoid repeating a punished response. Like reinforcement, the specific effects of punishment seem to depend on the circumstances in which it is experienced.

If the negative consequences are fairly mild or are presented only occasionally, we are less likely to change our behavior than if they are intense and experienced frequently. Also, if there are positive consequences associated with the punishment (for example, the respect and attention of one's peers for participating in a protest that leads to a fine), then the effect of the punishment will be less.

In conceptualizing how the Law of Effect works in specific situations, it is helpful to think of a scale with pleasant and aversive consequences opposing one another. The likelihood that the individual will continue to engage in an activity will depend on which is stronger, the positive force or the negative. As in interpersonal relationships, the ratio of cost to benefit is all-important. If punishment outweighs reinforcement, the behavior will stop; if not, it will continue but perhaps at a slower pace.

Most behavioral psychologists like to point out that punishment is not the only way that behavior is weakened and discouraged. There are at least two others. The first involves the weakening of behavior by the lack of sufficient reinforcement. If an activity no longer earns some sort of reinforcement, we'll stop doing it. Take the young man who stopped calling for a date because he never got a positive reply. He wasn't reinforced, so, after four tries, he quit. If, in the case of the eighteen-month-old who cried till his mother picked him up, she had ignored him and *not* picked him up, he would eventually have quit because he would no longer be getting reinforcement—mother's attention—for crying. (This assumes that such behavior is humanly possible on the part of the mother, which is doubtful.) Psychologists call this process *extinction.*

Behavior is extinguished when it is no longer followed by reinforcement. Unlike the results of punishment, the extinction process is fairly slow. It might take days or even weeks to get the eighteen-month-old baby to stop crying for attention if his mother ignores him. And in order for the extinction to be successful, the mother would have to make sure that he didn't get some other reinforcement for crying, like his grandfather's attention. But if he didn't get reinforcement, he would eventually learn. His mother's ignoring him would not affect his crying in other situations, as when he's hurt, for example. It would only affect his "crying for attention."

The other way that behavior is discouraged is to give reinforcement for the opposite behavior. We will certainly stop engaging in one activity if another activity produces greater reinforcement. And if the two are mutually incompatible, we'll drop the first altogether. If his mother taught him other ways to get her attention, the eighteen-month-old's crying would most likely diminish. She might encourage him to bring her a favorite book or toy for them to play with whenever he wants her attention—as well as discouraging his crying by ignoring it as much as possible.

This principle has helped many psychologists understand juvenile delinquency. Many unskilled adolescents turn to delinquent activities because they are unable to get the rewards in life by the socially accepted means. Since many of these young people lag far behind both educationally and socially, they cannot make it in the achievement-oriented, middle-class school environment. The socially acceptable middle-class way is just not an option for them. But they soon discover that they can get some of life's important reinforcers by turning to crime. Once they do this they usually find a delinquent subculture that will give them additional reinforcement in the form of status and prestige for their antisocial behavior. Illegal behavior quickly becomes a much more attractive alternative than school. Behavioral psychologists argue that we should turn the situation around by teaching these adolescents more acceptable ways to get the things they want. Rather than punishment, behaviorists recommend job training and more appropriate educational programs. Their idea is to give these young people training so that they'll have the skills to make it in our system. Not only are vocational and educational skills necessary, but so are the interpersonal skills of knowing how to get along effectively with other people. It seems fairly obvious that in order to make it in the middle-class game—in order to get into the game at all—these kids need to have all the ins and outs at their disposal.

However, just being adept at these particular skills is not enough. Here, too, one has to know *when* to use the skills in order for them to be effective. To begin with a simple example, let's return to the Skinner box. The professor is using a particular schedule of reinforcement to teach the rat to press the lever in a particular way. Now suppose the professor adds a little red light to the box. And suppose that no matter how correctly the rat performs his pressing task, he will never get reinforced for doing it unless he does it *when the light is on.* Very quickly the rat will learn that it makes no sense to press the lever when the light is off, and he'll stop doing it. But as soon as the light goes on, he'll start pressing because he knows that is the time when the pressing pays off. He has discriminated between the two situations—whether the light is on or off—and behaves accordingly. For this reason, psychologists call the red light a *discriminative stimulus*—a signal telling him whether he'll get reinforced.

Our lives are full of discriminative stimuli. People, places and situations often serve as discriminative stimuli. We quickly learn what kinds of behavior are expected in each situation. The sophisticated adolescent knows that swearing in front of his grandparents at the dinner table will be severely punished, whereas using the same words with his friends after school brings respect and status. The young child also makes these kinds of discriminations. If, for example, his father likes to roughhouse and lauds his son's fearless stunts but his mother gets upset and scolds him for playing rough, the child is likely to behave quite differently in the presence of each parent. He may be boisterous in the backyard with his father, but he settles down as soon as he notices his mother on the scene. The presence of each parent cues him to a behavior that will be reinforced. In the case of the employee who noticed his boss's disheveled appearance and irritability and postponed his request for a raise, the boss's appearance and actions served as discrimnative stimuli. He knew from past experience that when his boss was in such a mood, it was quite likely that he'd get punished for just about anything he did. And since he wanted to avoid a negative reaction to his request, he heeded the warning signals. Discriminative stimuli are clearly important for our survival.

Even finer discriminations than these occur in our everyday lives. When we know someone fairly well, the expression on his face alone is enough to enable us to predict how he'll react. Sometimes the cues we've learned are so subtle that we may not even be able to describe what they are, but they affect our behavior nonetheless. Two people who have been living together for a while can each tell pretty accurately when, and when not, a romantic overture is likely to meet with success—though each may not be able to explain exactly what it is about the other's behavior that lets him know it.

We often get into trouble when we misread discriminative stimuli. Much of our difficulties getting along in another culture involve our not understanding what different cues mean. We usually presume that they mean the same things as they do at home, but often they don't. The American traveler may expect that his overtures will be interpreted as signs of friendship and warmth when in fact they are often considered aggressive. To a great extent, our ability to get along with others depends upon our use of discriminative stimuli.

At first it may have sounded simple-minded—we do what feels good and we avoid doing things that hurt. But without going far beyond a basic explication of the Law of Effect, we have touched upon a number of important issues. The myriad ramifications of this law have direct relevance to almost every aspect of our lives.

Why Behaviorism?

The really striking difference between behaviorism and traditional psychology is the belief that psychological problems can be solved through the application of the principles we've just been discussing. Rather than analyzing dreams, delving into childhood conflicts and re-creating traumatic experiences, behaviorists try to improve the human condition by simply changing behavior.

According to traditional psychological and psychiatric thinking, "sick" behavior is always the symptom of some hidden conflict in the psyche. Behaviorists reject this notion because they find it more useful to regard the neurotic behavior itself as the problem. They believe that more adaptive, "healthy" behavior patterns can be *learned* to replace neurotic ("sick") ones; and they believe they can bring this about by training the client (patient) in certain specialized ways, without having to explore his psyche.

This point of view is, of course, the shocker that makes

many people regard behaviorism with contempt, if not horror, and as a cold and inhumanly scientific view of the nature of man. Because of the enormous influence Freud has had on contemporary thought, many of us have grown up with the notion that our behavior is the manifestation of conflicts between our id and superego, upon which our sanity depends; that our fears, our motivations, our problems with other people are all part of a complex, interwoven saga, much of it deeply buried, like a lost civilization. According to this view, we must probe our psyche carefully, peeling away the layers in order to understand ourselves. Only by doing this can we change.

Traditional psychiatric theory claims that if a purely behavioral strategy is employed in treating a problem, another problem will appear. Take the problem of insomnia, for example. According to traditional thinking, the insomnia merely indicates some underlying psychological disorder or conflict. In order to eliminate the problem, the underlying conflict must be resolved. If the problem behavior is somehow removed without resolving the conflict, then another symptom will replace the insomnia because the real "cause" of the problem still remains. If the person is taught some behavioral technique for falling asleep rapidly and doesn't go into lengthy psychological analysis, then another symptom, such as headaches or nail biting, will take its place. Only when the underlying disorder is resolved, this theory insists, can its outward manifestations be totally eliminated. According to this thesis, *symptom substitution* (as it is called by psychiatrists) would be inevitable when behaviorists treat people's problems.

The behaviorist's answer to this criticism is purely empirical: symptom substitution rarely, if ever, occurs. In their review of the literature, psychologists Leonard Ullmann and Leonard P. Krasner concluded that symptom substitution is the exception rather than the rule. Even many psychiatrists are now coming to the same conclusion; in fact, the members of a committee of the American Psychiatric Association recently informed its membership that they had found very few instances of symptom substitution, despite a careful search.

Behaviorists argue that new symptoms do not appear because all kinds of behavior, both normal and "pathological," are not symptoms at all. Rather, they are merely the individual's response to particular aspects of his environment. Particular maladaptive responses may have developed over a long period of time or may be reactions to immediate situations. If other maladaptive types of behavior *do* appear, it is likely that the individual is not currently being reinforced for using more desirable ones, possibly because he doesn't know how to carry them out, or because the individual's environment does not offer enough support for them. Thus, the psychotherapist must determine what factors in the person's "social environment" encourage the problem behavior and then rearrange things so that more adaptive ways of acting are encouraged.

Obviously this process is a lot simpler, more efficient and less painful than all that deep probing, and for this reason behaviorists feel they have wriggled free of the shackles of traditional psychological thinking. They *do* recognize the importance of attitudes and emotions, and *are* concerned about one's feelings of self-worth and self-concept—they simply do not make these things the focus of their work.

For the more radical behaviorists, like B. F. Skinner, feelings and emotions are by-products of reinforcement and punishment. For example, they believe that while we often give up when we're unhappy and depressed, it is not the sad feelings that make us quit. Rather, we are not getting enough reinforcement. The lack of reinforcement causes our depression as well as our quitting. Similarly, we try hard and feel confident if we succeed and receive rewards for our persistence. It is the reward, not our self-concept, that spurs us on.

Nonradical behaviorists, on the other hand, take a more moderate stance and argue that feelings and expectations affect what we do by influencing how we respond to particular rewards and punishments. A reward may be powerful or weak, depending upon how we feel when it is experienced. As mentioned before, behaviorists do not believe that our behavior is anything less than exceedingly complex. They believe that psychological problems can be solved better and more quickly if the focus is on what people actually do rather than on what they say about how they feel.

The movement of psychological thinking away from the rather poetic view of the human psyche as composed of layers of conflict and intrigue has been slow. During the first part of this century there were some who suggested that we should study human behavior rather than dreams and free associations. However, their impact was not great. Not until the late 1950's did behaviorism really begin to affect psychological practice. Since that time, behaviorism has become a dominant force in clinical psychology and psychiatry.

The reason for this great impact was that for the first time psychologists had a method that produced observable results. Using techniques derived from behavioral theory, psychologists could actually *see* big changes in the patients' behavior, and these breakthroughs coincided with the growing dissatisfaction among traditional psychotherapists with their own techniques.

Even though some people reported they felt better after talking with someone about their problems, controlled research failed to show that traditional one-to-one psychotherapy in a doctor's office was very beneficial. The results seemed to indicate that people got better or worse or stayed the same regardless of whether or not they received psychotherapy. British psychologist H. J. Eysenck presented the best-known investigation of the effectiveness of traditional psychotherapy. After examining the results of a wide variety of cases, Eysenck concluded that "There is no satisfactory evidence that psychotherapy benefits people suffering from neurotic conditions . . . The evidence fails to prove that psychotherapy, Freudian or otherwise, facilitates the recovery of neurotic patients."[1] The conclusions that Dr. Richard B. Stewart draws in his book *Trick or Treatment: How and Why Psychotherapy Fails,* are even more controversial. "In summary, it can be said that the patient who enters psychotherapy does so not without a distinct risk of deterioration or of simply wasting his time and money." ' Even though the validity of these conclusions has been questioned by professionals, they did much to encourage eager adoption of another approach to helping people cope with psychological problems.

The first published account of the use of behavioral techniques was in 1924 and involved the treatment of a three-year-old boy who had an intense fear of rabbits. The therapist was a young graduate student at Columbia University named Mary Cover Jones. No one knew why, but the child showed severe anxiety, even crying, when in the presence of a variety of furry objects, including fur coats, wool rugs, feathers and small animals, especially rabbits. Jones did not use deep and lengthy Freudian probing into the child's unconscious to discover the hidden origin of his fears. Instead, she took the basic learning principles we've described and simply taught him not to be afraid.

She started out by presenting him with the rabbit in a way that did *not* frighten him. While he was eating some of his favorite foods in a comfortable situation she had the rabbit placed, in a cage, far enough away from him so that although he was aware of its presence, it was not alarming enough to interfere with his enjoyment of the food. Every day the rabbit was moved just a little bit closer, but never close enough to be frightening. Eventually it was let out of the cage and gradually brought close to the child. By the end of treatment he was even able to play with it affectionately.

The child had learned to associate the rabbit with the pleasurable activity of eating. He learned that the rabbit wasn't going to hurt him, he saw other children playing happily with it, and his fear was simply wiped out—as was his fear of other furry objects. This procedure is straightforward, really nothing more than a systematic application of common sense: introduce the feared object very gradually, while making sure that the fearful person is calm and relaxed throughout.

Another interesting early example of the application of learning principles to psychological problems involves the treatment of enuresis, or bed-wetting. The Freudians had (and, in fact, still have) plenty of fascinating explanations for this particular problem. It has been interpreted as a demand for love, a "weeping through the bladder," as well as a form of aggression toward the parents. In his text on neurosis, O. Fenichel explains bed-wetting as "an expression of sexual fantasies proper to the opposite sex. Girls in whom urethral eroticism is well marked are almost always dominated by an intense envy of the penis. Their symptom (bed-wetting) gives expression to the wish to urinate like a boy. In boys the incontinence usually has the meaning of a female trait; such boys hope to obtain female kinds of pleasure by 'urinating passively.' "[3]

Two early behaviorists, Hobart and Molly Mowrer, dispensed with all of that and treated bed-wetting as merely the child's inability to control his bladder. Whatever the reason, he just hadn't learned how to control it, and their objective was to teach him to do so. They designed a pad that was placed on the bed or in the child's pants and sounded a buzzer when any moisture touched it. In other words, as soon as he began to urinate, the buzzer would sound and continue until the child woke up and turned it off. Through repeated associations of the distended bladder and awakening, the child learned to wake up rather than void in response to the sensation of a full bladder. This method was very successful in "curing" enuresis to the point that the child learned to hold his urine through the night. What's more, the procedure works very fast and is inexpensive. In fact, a similarly designed apparatus is available in the Sears catalogue. The original technique has been slightly modified in the last thirty-five years, but the principles involved have not.

Behaviorists now look back on the work of Jones and the Mowrers as classic examples of their approach, but at the time the reports were published, their efforts were not recognized as revolutionary. By March 1938 there were over twenty-five published accounts of the application of behavior theory in the treatment of problems ranging from children's fears to adult depression and alcoholism. Still, not until psychologists grew disenchanted with traditional psychotherapy did behaviorism really begin having an impact on psychiatric theory and practice. The terms "behavior modification" and "behavior therapy" weren't even part of psychological jargon until the last decade.

The modern origins of behavior modification can be traced to at least two independent sources. One group, Skinner and his associates, were experimental psychologists studying the behavior of animals in laboratory situations. They were interested in finding out whether the behavioral principles they had discovered applied as well to the activities of psychotic patients in mental institutions. The other group, psychiatrists and clinical psychologists, wanted to develop ways to become more effective with their patients. During the late fifties these therapists, working in South Africa and at the Maudsley Hospital in London, began looking toward experimental psychology for suggestions. Their idea was to use methods based on learning principles along with traditional psychotherapy techniques. In 1958 Joseph Wolpe, then a psychiatrist in South Africa, introduced behavioral techniques that proved extremely effective in dealing with people's irrational fears and phobias.

Rather than trying to remove the phobia by analyzing its possible symbolic meaning, Wolpe suggested that conditioning would better eliminate anxiety reactions. The conditioning process begins with the therapist teaching the client a certain kind of behavior that is incompatible with anxiety. For example, a patient may be systematically taught how to relax every muscle in his body in order to achieve a deep state of relaxation. When the patient has learned how to relax completely at will, the therapist asks him to do so while imagining the least frightening aspect of the feared situation. If the patient is especially anxious about being in large crowds, for example, the therapist may ask him to imagine seeing a small gathering of people in the distance. Once the patient is able to maintain the state of relaxation while imagining such a scene, he may be asked to imagine himself closer to the crowd. When the patient is finally able to remain relaxed even when he is imagining the most frightening aspects of the situation, he should no longer experience anxiety. Since it is functionally impossible for a person to suffer anxiety when he is relaxed, Wolpe reasoned that the pairing of the feared situation with relaxation would eliminate the anxiety reaction. Although Wolpe's method, known as *reciprocal inhibition,* has been refined since it was first introduced almost twenty years ago, many aspects of his techniques have proven quite effective in treating people suffering from severe anxiety.

Unknown to Wolpe and his colleagues in South Africa and Great Britain, Skinner and his associates in the United States were also investigating the application of behavior principles to psychological problems. Their initial goal was to determine how psychotic individuals respond to reinforcement and to see if their behavior would change in relation to how the reinforcers were delivered. Like most laboratory psychologists, they began with a very simple response that they could easily observe and measure. The patients were seated in a small room behind levers that produced candy and treats when pressed. By recording when and how often they pressed the lever in relation to how the lever was programmed to produce reinforcers, the psychologist were able to analyze the patients' behavior. To the amazement of many, Skinner's laboratory results were confirmed: the psychotic patients' behavior was predictable.

Following this rather theoretical research in the early fifties, Skinner and his co-workers moved in to study behaviors that had more therapeutic significance. Child psychologist Sidney Bijou and a group of psychologists and teachers at the University of Washington started testing some of these ideas with young children who had been referred for special help. Their strategy was to devise ways of motivating these children to behave in more appropriate ways, and their primary "tools" were praise from adults and M & M chocolate candy. There was one severely withdrawn nursery-school girl who would not play with any other children and who spent 90 percent of the day crawling around the floor, even though she was perfectly able to walk. Rather than going into lengthy psychotherapy and analysis, the teachers started making sure that she received lots of praise and attention every time she even moved toward another child or off the floor for an instant. They did not plead with her to play or cajole her into being happy when she was withdrawn because they felt that such reactions on their part might serve to encourage and actually reward her for being withdrawn. To the delight of the staff her condition improved dramatically. As she began moving more into the group the teachers started expecting more from her and praised her for her progress. Within a relatively short period of time the girl actively participated in the classroom and enjoyed all that the school had to offer. They used the same techniques with a severely disturbed six-year-old boy to eliminate his temper tantrums and self-injurious acts. Essentially what they did was to reward him lavishly for engaging in constructive activities while totally ignoring him whenever he had a tantrum. It worked; with a great deal of training and "therapy" his behavior improved so that he was able to attend a regular elementary school. The success that they had with these and other problem children prompted them to extend their work into the treatment of mentally retarded and schizophrenic children. At about the same time that Bijou and his group at Washington were trying out these new methods, other psychologists in the United States and Canada were experiencing success using the techniques with both adults and children. It was clear that they had come upon something effective.

Both Wolpe and Skinner were interested in finding a name for their techniques, and interestingly enough, their groups came up with the same name quite independently. They wanted a term that clearly acknowledged their split from traditional psychiatry and at the same time expressed their goal of helping disturbed people. In 1953 Skinner and his student Ogden Lindsley came up with the term "behavior therapy," to refer to the treatment of behavior problems. The term was good because it specified both the focus and the purpose of their new methods.

Since the late fifties the term "behavior modification" has been used interchangeably with behavior therapy. And almost every textbook on clinical psychology and psychiatry has offered slightly differing definitions of each of these terms. For convenience, we will make a distinction between the two and will use the definitions found in the most recent edition of the *American Handbook of Psychiatry*. Behavior *modification* refers to the application of behavior principles to many human situations, including child rearing, education, psychotherapy, vocational preparation, business, and social movements. Behavior *therapy* is the application of these principles to the psychological problems, disturbances and disorders in children and adults.

As it has turned out, these terms were not such a good selection. While they may have very specific meanings to psychologists and other professionals and refer to particular methods derived from the behavioral tradition within academic circles, their dictionary definitions are much more general. The terms literally included all methods used to change behavior—psychosurgery, drugs and torture, as well as psychotherapy based on empirically derived principles of behavior. Because of this situation many laymen and journalists have looked on behavior modification with suspicion and horror. It seems clear that the terms need some modification themselves. In order to set things straight and to "clean up" behavioral psychologists' reputation, there has been a recent move to stop using the terms. In the last year two reports, one from the National Institutes of Mental Health and the other from the American Psychological Association, have avoided the terms altogether. Some behaviorists have suggested the term "applied behavior analysis," and others the term "environment modification." But these may also introduce confusion without accurately reflecting everything that behaviorists do.

It looks as if psychology is left with the terms "behavior modification" and "behavior therapy," and all that psychologists can do to clear up the confusion is to try to explain exactly what they do when they apply behavioral principles to people's problems.

IV

Getting Along with People: From Child Rearing to Assertiveness Training

Many psychologists believe that success in interpersonal relations depends upon how we apply principles of behavior modification in our daily lives. Although behaviorists readily admit that they do not have immediate solutions to all interpersonal conflict, they have discovered certain things we can do to help us get along better with each other.

In this chapter we will focus on techniques for getting along better with both children and adults. Let's start with the common and often bewildering business of bringing up one's own children. In this area behavioral psychologists have really gotten into the act. Their numerous "how-to-do-it" manuals are intended to give parents an understanding of behavioral principles and to point out how parents and children influence one another's behavior. These books emphasize the fact that parents *are* behavior modifiers whether they know it or not, and that it is to everyone's advantage for parents to deal with their children more effectively.

While each manual follows a slightly different format, all

focus on two basic techniques: reinforcement and something they call "timeout." Parents are urged to consider the actions of their children in terms of the benefits that each behavior brings the child. Does Johnny's crying and tantrums result in your giving him your immediate attention? Do you give him candy in the supermarket to keep him happy and to prevent him from making a scene? What happens when he sits quietly playing with his toys? Without even realizing it, parents, as we have seen, may actually be encouraging their child's misbehavior.

Parental attention is usually a strong reward for the child. The attention reinforces the behavior that got it for him. But when does the child get attention? Most often it's *not* when he's behaving well—playing quietly, for example—because very naturally, that's when parents have the chance to get other things done and leave the child alone. The manuals point out, however, that that is exactly when the parents *should* be giving the child at least some attention, since that is when this strong reward will serve to encourage the good behavior. By giving their child their greatest attention when he fusses or gets into mischief, parents are actually rewarding him for misbehaving —and letting him know that misbehaving is going to get him what he wants.

This way of looking at the child's behavior often makes the child's actions seem quite reasonable. What child wouldn't fuss if fussing were the best way (if not, indeed, the only way) to get his parents' undivided attention? Behaviorists contend that children don't misbehave because they're "bad" or because they're responding to deep psychological complexes, but because misbehaving pays off better than being good. Just try to remember the last time you gave your child a special treat for playing quietly or sharing his toys with a playmate. Since we *expect* our children to behave well, we don't very often make a big deal about it when they do. And according to behavior modification, it is totally inappropriate to respond to the child when he misbehaves and ignore him when his behavior is good. In order to change the child's way of acting, so the theory goes, we must change the way we react.

Sometimes parents just need to be reminded to take notice of good behavior. To this end, psychologists Emily Herbert and Donald Baer of the University of Kansas gave mothers of problem children golfer's wrist counters and told them to press the counter each time they took special notice of their child's good behavior. Interestingly enough, as soon as they started recording how they interacted with their child, they became more positive and their child's behavior improved. Not only did the children become more cooperative, but their tantrums and aggressiveness diminished. When the psychologists checked in on the families eight months later, things were still going well. Both mothers and children were pleased with the changes and there were no new problems. As with many families, lengthy and expensive counseling and special training were not necessary. The parents simply needed a reminder to do something they already knew how to do.

Using positive reinforcement also results in some very important spin-offs. It tends to change the whole atmosphere of the family. Not only does one pleasant comment usually lead to a pleasant comment in return, but the child's general attitude toward the parents also improves. As one might expect, children prefer and seek out adults who make their wishes clear and respond enthusiastically. What's more, the view of their child seems to change when the parents start focusing on good behavior. Often they are surprised at how well behaved their child really is.

It is important to emphasize that behavior modifiers are not telling parents to be positive and to dispense goodies no matter what the child does. The praise and attention are supposed to be given only when the child is well behaved. If a child is rewarded regardless of how he acts, his behavior will not improve, and in fact, may get worse. In such cases the Law of Effect may work against the parents and child. Psychologists Herbert and Baer asked mothers to record when they responded to their child's *good behavior* in a positive way, not just any time that they were positive with their child. Like any good behavior modifiers, parents must be quite clear about what behavior to encourage. And they must follow through consistently. The essential point is to reward the child when he behaves in a desirable manner—not only when he does something outstanding, but also for ordinary, everyday little things—and he will begin to behave that way more often.

What we've just been saying about dealing with children is equally valid in terms of our relationships with adults. Obviously it is very important to be positive, but that does not mean it cannot backfire. One can get carried away and throw praise and compliments around too freely—with very disappointing results. We're all familiar with people who are too positive—an unkind word never crosses their lips, they smile all the time, they love everybody—and we tend to find them boring, if not sickening. Even worse, we eventually stop listening to them. If a salesman in a clothing store tells us that everything we try on looks great, we'll quickly stop paying attention to what he says, assume he's just trying to make a sale, and probably get annoyed and leave the store without buying anything. In our personal life it may be pleasant at first to get involved with someone who's always telling us how wonderful we are and who responds to everything we say and do with bubbling enthusiasm, but it won't be long before we suspect that his compliments are empty and serve some ulterior motive. Like the boy who cried wolf, such people quickly lose credibility and our response to them tends to be either indifference or hostility.

What they are doing, in behavioral terms, is delivering *noncontingent* reinforcement—and free reinforcement given regardless of what someone does is, at best, useless. To be effective and meaningful, our positive comments must be specifically related to the behavior of the person we give them to. This means being honest and giving praise and approval only when we mean it—but it does not mean being stingy with praise. Even if the person with whom we're dealing is frequently inept, we can still be positive without being insincere (i.e., noncontingent). Sometimes we must even show the person what to do so that we can reward him. Rather than criticizing someone most of the time and then not noticing when he's done something right, we should include within our criticism suggestions for doing better and then let the person know when he's done well. If we do this, he is likely to improve and be happier with himself as well.

But this is only half the story. As nice as all this sounds, it is obvious that there are situations with both adults and children in which only being positive won't work.

To go back to the issue of child rearing. Okay, so you reward your child when he is trustworthy, loyal, helpful, friendly, courteous, kind, obedient, cheerful, thrifty, brave, clean and reverent. But how about when he's destructive, cruel, selfish, loud and a pest? (Children have been known to exhibit such behavior.) The natural reaction is to ask him to stop, to beg him to stop, to order him to stop; and then, if he doesn't stop, to either give in to him or give him a spanking, thereby escalating the level of unpleasantness in the environment— none of which, we can all agree, is a particularly constructive way of handling the situation.

Again, applying the Law of Effect, the behaviorist would advise one to ignore the child's misbehavior. Many children misbehave because it gets them lots of attention, and as we have said before, adult attention, regardless of how it is intended, is usually a powerful reward for children. Research studies on children in schools have proved that reprimands can sometimes function as a positive payoff. In one study a first-grade teacher was able to reduce the misbehavior of her pupils by merely ignoring the children whenever they misbehaved rather than scolding them. Assuming that children behave in a particular way in order to get a response from adults, then if parents stop giving attention to such antics, much of the children's motivation for misbehaving will be eliminated.

At least theoretically, if parents are able to make good behavior really pay off, so that it is a more attractive alternative than misbehavior, then misbehavior should diminish if the parents consistently ignore it. Good behavior should smother misbehavior if things are set up right. According to psychologists, the ideal situation would be for all behavior modification to be accomplished by using only positive reinforcement and by directing all efforts toward increasing positive behavior.

We need hardly explain that certain problems may arise when this theory is put into practice. In the first place, the desire for attention is *not* the only reason why children misbehave, and if attention is not what a child is after, then merely withholding attention is irrelevant to the behavior and will not affect it. But even if he is seeking attention, there are still many situations in which ignoring him simply will not work. You may well be reinforcing your son's bashing-at-the-stereo-with-a-baseball-bat behavior by giving him the attention of shrieking and dragging him away from the thing, but nevertheless you do want to protect the equipment, and just sitting there calmly and ignoring what is happening will not suffice. To take a less extreme example, it just is not feasible to ignore a child who follows you around all day whining, or who consistently picks on his little sister. You cannot ignore him; you have got to stop him. And one alternative that comes very quickly to mind is punishment.

Aha, punishment! As we suggested earlier, there is no topic that is more taboo in behavior modification. It is inevitable that most parents are going to feel the need to make use of punishment at times; yet most of those parent training manuals do not even mention it and the ones that do discourage its use. There are at least three reasons for this strong opposition to punishment. First, inflicting pain is distasteful to most people, and behavior psychologists are no exception; they do not like the idea of punishing people in order to modify their behavior. Second, many fear that punishment may lead to serious consequences, or "side effects." The child may become very upset, cry and may not get back to normal for some time. Another fear is that someone who is punished may come to avoid those people and situations he associates with punishment. The child who is severely and repeatedly punished by his parents may come to resent and fear them and even run away from them. Or the child may try to figure out ways to avoid his parents' punishment. He may lie or hide the "evidence."

So behaviorists do not recommend punishment. They also tell us that giving the child attention, or any other reward, to get him to stop misbehaving only teaches him to misbehave more often. So what do they advise parents to do when their child starts breaking up the stereo, picking on his sister or doing something else that just cannot be ignored?

One answer is the behavioral technique known as *timeout.* Timeout consists of briefly removing someone from a situation in which he can get reinforcement. It is, in fact, the opposite of reinforcement. Take the example of the child who keeps picking on his sister and won't leave her alone. To use timeout the parents, without yelling or getting upset, may put the child in a chair in the corner of the room. The parents would not give him any toys or let him watch TV, and no one would talk to him. The child would just have to sit alone *for a short while.* If the parents find that the child will not stay in the chair without scolding or force, then timeout may involve removing the child from the scene and putting him in a nonthreatening place where there is no source of reinforcement. They might put him in a room by himself, and if necessary, shut the door. The isolation and lack of access to TV, toys and attention constitute a timeout from reinforcement; that is, the availability of reward is taken away for a period of time. And the effect of timeout is the opposite of reinforcement: it discourages whatever behavior earned it.

Timeout allows the parents to stop the behavior without using punishment, and at the same time discourages the child from behaving that way in the future. To be maximally effective, timeout must be used in conjunction with positive reinforcement. In this way, not only will the child be discouraged from misbehaving by the loss of reinforcement, but he will also be encouraged to behave better by being reinforced when he does.

Let us look at an actual case to see how all this works. Two sets of parents had young school-aged boys they could not cope with. The boys were stubborn and negative, threw tantrums, refused to cooperate with their parents or follow instructions.

Since their many attempts at reasoning with the boys hadn't worked, the parents ended up vacillating between letting the children have their own way and resorting to spankings, a system that did nothing to improve their behavior. Finally they brought the boys to a local mental-health clinic. After observing the children and parents interacting with one another, psychologist Robert Wahler instructed the parents in the use of behavior modification. The parents were specifically taught how to identify good behavior and how to use positive reinforcement and timeout—to give lots of praise and approval whenever the boys were cooperative, and to isolate them in their bedrooms for five minutes when they were disobedient. Whenever the child began to throw a tantrum or refused to mind, they were to take him immediately to his room without arguing or getting upset. Whenever he cooperated, he was to receive immediate praise. Both boys reacted well to their parents' new ways of responding to them—their misbehavior diminished. Moreover, both parents and children appeared better off in other ways. The parents reported that they liked being with their child more, and the two boys had a more positive attitude toward their parents. Clearly, a positive "snowball" developed after the parents learned to be more effective behavior modifiers.

The behavioral methods for dealing with children when they're doing something we do not want them to do can also be used with adults. We can leave the room, pick up the newspaper or act uninterested when our mate starts nagging. But there are situations in which timeout is impossible or not effective enough. Sometimes we have to do more than just withhold reinforcement: we have to say things that people do not want to hear.

And yet most of us are reluctant to give negative feedback. We worry that our negative comments may make people dislike us or avoid us in the future. We may even fear that our criticism will evoke aggression and a black eye. Even though it is usually ridiculous to think that one criticism could have such disastrous results, we still fear what others might do if we really expressed our honest feelings.

Behaviorists recommend that we confine our negative remarks to specific actions or events we do not like rather than using them as a general criticism of the person. Instead of saying, for example, "Can't you ever do anything right?" or "You jerk, you're so stupid that you can't even add," it would be better to say, "Do you think there's a better way to do that?" or "You added my bill incorrectly." And if the response you get is, "Are you calling me stupid?" you can reply, "No, I just think there is some mistake." Certainly a criticism of a particular thing someone has done is far less insulting and irritating than a condemnation of the entire person.

Another way to prevent unwanted repercussions is to make criticism constructive; that is, to include within the criticism suggestions as to what the person might do to correct the problem. Providing a solution makes it possible for the person to know what to do in the future. In behavioral terms, constructive comments serve to *prompt* a behavior that will bring reinforcement. If all he gets is complaints, the person may have no way of knowing what he's supposed to do, or how to improve. Take, for example, the process of learning a sport, any sport. If your tennis coach yells at you each time you serve but doesn't show you how to do it correctly, you may continue to do it wrong or get it right only by trial and error. If so, chances are you will quit tennis before you ever learn to play. But if the coach tells you exactly what's wrong with your serve and how to do it right, you will be better able to improve and avoid his criticism. In situations where negative reactions are constructive, you may very well appreciate the help.

Even so, understanding perfectly well how to express negative feelings without causing conflict and tension does not mean being able to carry it off successfully when we are faced with a real-life situation. We feel uneasy when we have to tell people that they have failed or that we don't like what they have done; we feel guilty when we have to say no. There are, in fact, some people who avoid dissension at all costs. In situations where their needs and desires are incompatible with what someone else wants, they say nothing. Or they may be so uncomfortable about expressing their desires that they wait until the pressure becomes unbearable and then they explode.

Consider Mime and Alberich, the dwarf brothers in Wagner's *Ring* operas. Mime is timid and obsequious; he cannot express his own needs directly and never tells anyone how he really feels. He is always positive on the outside, though inside he loathes everyone for mistreating him; and of course everyone sees through his noncontingent use of positive reinforcement and treats him with more contempt than ever, which only makes him all the more bitter. In the end he is cut up in little pieces by the heroic youth he has spent his life bringing up, a man who hates him more than anyone else. Mime's brother Alberich, on the other hand, lacks the appropriate social skills to deal diplomatically with other people. He cannot express his needs either, but instead of covering them up, he gets angry and grabs things, yells at people and puts curses on them. Though he briefly achieves a position of power, he cannot get along with anyone either and ends up losing everything, and being called a toad. Both would have been better off if they had had access to what psychologists call *assertiveness training*.

Assertiveness training is a technique for teaching people how to express their needs and feelings in ways that do not have unpleasant repercussions. Assertiveness is *not* synonymous with aggressive behavior—assertive behavior is an honest and socially appropriate expression of feelings, whether they be positive or negative. There are definite benefits to possessing this skill. An assertive person is more likely to have a satisfying life because he is better equipped to get what he wants out of life, both socially and materially. Evidence also exists that assertive behavior instills a feeling of well-being in a person. A major source of anxiety may be eliminated when one no longer fears repercussions from expressing his needs and feelings honestly.

A newcomer to a swinging Manhattan singles bar may

find herself spending an evening with a bore, giving him her telephone number and perhaps even accepting his sexual advances. She may hate herself, she may be extremely upset, but she doesn't have the courage to say no. A nonassertive student might put up with people carrying on a loud conversation in a crowded library, making it impossible for him to work. He would most likely just sit there miserably, waiting for them to stop.

While this extreme passivity may make it possible to avoid interpersonal conflict, nonassertive people usually lose in the long run. Their needs are not being met and this makes them feel frustrated and resentful. Women in particular often find themselves in this kind of trap, a fact that is one of the significant issues of the women's liberation movement. Many women find that their primary function in life is to satisfy the needs of the rest of the family. What liberation means in this situation is the woman's asserting her right to meet her own needs.

Other individuals are able to express their needs but do it in ways that evoke negative and aggressive reactions from others. Rather than calmly asking the people upstairs to keep their party a little quieter, this kind of person would wait and fume until it was three in the morning and he was in a tearing rage. Then he might rush upstairs in his robe, bang on the door and yell that he was calling the cops. Not only is he allowing the situation to make him miserable, he is also making a fool of himself. The people upstairs will certainly think he's peculiar and might also get angry. In contrast to being victimized like the overly submissive individual, this person may well end up alienating himself from practically everyone.

Some people have difficulty expressing positive feelings. They want the one they love to "just understand." They think they "don't have to tell you how I feel." The implication is that it is somehow the "responsibility" of the one who is close to know that he or she is loved. But people cannot read minds, no matter how long they have lived with someone. Obviously, when positive emotions are not explicitly communicated, frustration and misunderstanding will occur. The love-means-never-having-to-say-you're-sorry philosophy can be very destructive.

One difficulty in helping the kind of people we have been discussing is that they are frequently unaware of their problem. They sense something is wrong; they're anxious, upset or frustrated in their relationships with others, but they cannot specifically identify what has to be changed. The therapist, however, can often see indications of unexpressed emotions, interpersonal anxiety or habitual avoidance of important confrontations, and if so, he might consider using assertiveness training. Of course, it often takes a long time for these people to be able to understand what their problem is. But assertiveness training cannot begin until the client does understand.

Whether or not a person acts assertively often depends upon the situation. A woman may be perfectly capable of expressing her needs to her husband and still be victimized by her boss. She may be able to discipline her children effectively, yet be unable to deal with a waitress who has overcharged her. A businessman can be murder at the bargaining table and then wilt when his domineering mother starts making unreasonable demands. Thus, the therapist's assessment of his patient's problem will include a determination of the situations in which lack of assertiveness is a major factor.

The patient begins by practicing remedial skills in the therapist's office. With the therapist playing the role of a significant person in the client's life, certain conflicts are re-enacted. Because the therapist has spent a great deal of time talking with his client, he is able to assume many of the characteristics of the person or people the client has trouble dealing with. Sometimes the therapist decides to be stubborn and hostile in his role playing so that the client can have extra practice handling especially uncomfortable situations. If the client has difficulty, the therapist stops and immediately suggests better ways to handle the problem.

As with all behavior programs, the therapist begins with relatively simple situations and dispenses lots of reinforcement for the client's progress. Once he is able to handle milder conflicts, they move on to situations that cause more anxiety. In these role-playing sessions the therapist demonstrates how the client can express his feelings without generating repercussions.

When the therapist feels that the client is comfortable with the techniques, he begins to teach him what to do in situations in which the conflict is not resolved by his first assertive response. The client is taught to provide additional justification for his position if the initial statements don't work. Say the client is in a movie theater and the people in front of him ignore his first polite request that they be quiet. After waiting a few minutes he might ask them again and add that he cannot hear the movie dialogue. If they still continue to talk, he might finally threaten to call the manager. Of course, the therapist explains that most people usually comply with a single request, but that the client should be prepared to handle a variety of situations.

The therapist will also give his client assignments so that he can begin to try out his skills in real-life situations. As with his earlier training, the assignments would be simple at first but would become more demanding as his skills increase.

Assertiveness training is often conducted in groups. Before the group begins meeting, the therapist selects clients for whom assertiveness training seems appropriate. Following the format we have just discussed, the therapist might begin by having the group members discuss their interpersonal problems. Once all of the members recognize their problems, the therapist could start role playing. By having a group of people rather than only one therapist to provide feedback to the individual, he can learn to be even more confident about the effect of his assertiveness in real-life situations.

As we mentioned earlier, assertiveness training is also used with individuals who come across as hostile and inconsiderate when they express their feelings. Impulsive, aggressive people often cause themselves and others greater pain and unhappiness than people who are overly submissive. What they say often gets them into trouble. They don't discuss, they argue;

they don't request, they demand. When a waitress brings the wrong order to a man like this, he tells her how stupid she is. If someone bumps into him in a crowded subway station, he tells him to get the hell out of the way. Or he may be calm around everyone but his brother-in-law. When they get together he becomes nasty and sarcastic and tries to make a fool out of the guy. The behavior of these people is clearly inappropriate and rarely helps them get what they want. Even if they succeed in achieving their goal, they still cause a great deal of unhappiness to others.

Though such people seem to be the direct opposite of nonassertive individuals, assertiveness training can be helpful for them as well. For both kinds of people, the goal of treatment—appropriate and effective expression of feelings—is the same. The therapist, however, starts from a different place. The aggressive individual already knows that there is nothing wrong with expressing his needs and in most cases he also knows what it is that has to be changed. So the therapist can start right in with the role playing, training the client to express himself more skillfully. From this point on, the techniques are very similar to those we've outlined for the nonassertive person —practicing the skills with the therapist and then trying them out in real life.

Essentially, assertiveness training involves learning how to express negative as well as positive feelings in ways that will be accepted by others. It teaches people to get greater reinforcement. By being effectively assertive, people are mastering the Law of Effect to their own advantage. And since this skill makes them better able to deal with other people, everyone is better off.

Perhaps the most convincing example of the benefits of harnessing the Law of Effect in our relations with other people is what happened to a group of seven junior high school students in Visalia, California. These boys were incorrigible, the worst troublemakers in the school. When their teachers were told that a special class was being set up for "difficult" students, they were only too happy to let the troublemakers attend. But what the boys learned in the class was more than just how to be "well behaved."

The prevailing atmosphere in this school was one of tough discipline, and many of the teachers were quite authoritarian. The Director of Special Education for the school system, Harry Rosenberg, and a consulting psychologist, Paul Graubard, decided that what these boys needed was not more discipline, but training in how to deal with teachers and other adult authority figures more effectively. If the boys understood behavioral principles and were more positive in their reactions to teachers, then the teachers would in turn relate to them more positively. To accomplish this, Rosenberg and Graubard gave these teenagers instruction in behavior modification for one class period each day.

In addition to learning how reinforcement and timeout work, they were taught how to reward their teachers for being nicer to them. When a teacher was friendly or gave them a little extra help, they let her know they appreciated it. "Gee, that's interesting," they would say, looking the teacher straight in the eye after she had patiently explained a point, or "You really help me learn when you explain things that way." They were also taught that it is important to be sincere, to make their positive comments contingent upon desired behavior. And when a teacher yelled at them or treated them unfairly, they were instructed not to holler back or glare at the teacher, but instead just look away from the teacher and avoid eye contact.

The boys practiced saying nice things and then listened to how they sounded on a tape recorder. And one boy had to work on smiling. Even though his smile was a genuine expression of his satisfaction and appreciation, it was interpreted by his teachers as a sneer and they usually reacted accordingly. So he practiced smiling in front of a mirror until his facial expression communicated positive feelings more clearly. The boys also did some role playing in which they took turns being the teacher and seeing how they might react to people like themselves. Two of the most important things that they learned in the course were how to be more responsive to nonverbal communication and how to predict what others might do in certain situations.

In order to get an absolutely accurate measurement of how the program worked, the therapists gave the boys golfer's wrist counters and instructed them to record the number of positive and negative interactions with the teachers. As the boys perfected their new techniques, the number of positive incidents went way up, and the number of negative contacts actually dropped to zero. The course was a fantastic success. Teachers and students began liking one another more, and the boys who participated felt that they had more power in their relationships with their teachers. In a very real sense, they did.

Graubard and Rosenberg did wonder if they were training these boys to be superior con artists. It's true that there were some students who were not absolutely sincere in their use of these techniques. Still, none of the students was really getting away with anything, since the benefits were clearly felt by the teachers as well as the students. The next result was a decrease in the violence and disruption that had previously characterized the students' classroom behavior. This change benefited everyone.

The program worked so well that the school system has continued to use it to train many different types of students. It turned out that many of the more successful students did not need to be taught to use behavior modification at all. When they were told what the principles were, these students explained that they already used them quite naturally. It was simply the best way to get along with the teachers.

They were right.

Actually, the behavioral approach to getting along with others is a more sophisticated version of axioms repeated many times by the Bible, Ann Landers and Bertrand Russell.

V

Self-Control: At the Refrigerator, in the Smoking Lounge and at the Biofeedback Machine

It is a rare person who has not at some time grappled with the problem of resisting temptation. Examples are all too familiar: refusing that piece of rich pastry; finishing your income-tax forms after dinner rather than collapsing in front of the TV; trying to stop smoking. Alexander Woollcott's observation that "all the things I really like to do are either immoral, illegal or fattening" is one way of describing the problem of self-control. The behaviorist, as usual, would be a bit more precise, characterizing the above examples as types of behavior that immediately gratify but result in long-term negative consequences. (In other words, the pastry is delicious, but will make you fat, and so on.) The difficulty is that the present is always more real than the future; it's easy to tell ourselves that this is the last time, that it will never happen again. But all too often it does happen again. Certainly it would be a tremendous boon to mankind if someone could come up with a way to make it easy to resist temptation.

Don't hold your breath; no such magic seems possible even in the remotely foreseeable future. The spirit is willing but the flesh is weak, and so on. However, behavioral techniques are now being developed that do make it easier (if not exactly easy) to resist temptation—and that seem to be particularly successful in dealing with some of these problems. And we might as well start with the problem common to millions of Americans, a problem that is talked and written about endlessly —weight control and obesity. Fortunately, behavior modification has something new to say about it.

It is a sad fact but regrettably true that overweight people spend a large part of their lives agonizingly trying to get thin and hardly ever succeeding. According to behavioral therapist Richard Stuart and nutritionist Barbara Davis, the average overweight person goes on 1.5 diets a year and makes over 15 major attempts to lose weight between the ages of twenty-one and fifty. Most of them fail. Stanford University psychiatrist A. J. Stunkard reports that most overweight people do not even seek professional treatment and those who do often drop out without losing much weight. "To qualify this dismal tale," he goes on, "we surveyed the medical literature and summarized the results of treatment for obesity. We took all reports in a 10-year period and calculated what percentages of patients who entered treatment lost significant amounts of weight. There was a remarkable unanimity in these results. No more than 25% of the patients lost as much as 20 pounds and no more than 5% lost as much as 40 pounds. That is not a very good record."[1] Moreover, those who somehow manage to lose the unwanted weight usually gain all of it back in a short period of time.

Obviously, then, the traditional dietary, pharmaceutical and psychotherapeutic approaches to obesity are not very effective. Regardless of those before-and-after photos in magazine ads, or the fervent claims of the latest fad-diet book, most of us fail miserably at losing weight. But those methods are no longer the overweight person's only recourse. Behavior-modification procedures are now being used to treat the problem of obesity and the results are promising. The technique involves the overweight person learning methods of self-control to modify his own eating "behavior"; it is the individual himself who actually carries out his behavior-modification program.

Most biological scientists and physicians agree that the major cause of obesity is simply overeating; there is an excess of caloric intake in relation to energy expended. Although medical authorities realize that different people require different amounts of food to maintain the same weight, glandular abnormality is rarely the cause of obesity. Another fact that serves as a basis for the behavioral approach to weight control is that much of eating is controlled by the environment. We often eat not because we are hungry or are in need of nourishment, but because it is "time to eat." There are also situations in which eating is expected of us—when we are at a party, for example, or in an ice cream parlor—and there are times when eating is the best entertainment available, such as a long evening at home when there is nothing better to do than have another bowl of ice cream. What we must do to avoid overeating is try to achieve what is called *situational control.*

We can credit psychologist Charles B. Ferster of American University and his colleagues J. I. Nurnberger and E. E. Levitt with first conceptualizing obesity and weight control as problems of behavior management and self-control. In 1962 they published a detailed analysis of the influence of situational factors in weight control. Five years later Richard Stuart reported a remarkable series of case studies incorporating Ferster's procedures. All of his patients who remained in treatment (only 20 percent dropped out) lost at least thirty pounds, and 30 percent lost more than forty pounds within twelve months. These results were by far the most outstanding ever reported for the treatment of obesity, and subsequent experimental research by psychologist Janet Wollersheim confirmed the effectiveness of behavior modification in this area.

What a behavioral self-control program amounts to is radically changing the person's entire relationship to food. Other approaches merely try to change a person's weight instead of changing his ingrained patterns of eating. But no matter how thin we get by crash diets or appetite-suppressing drugs, we'll most likely become fat again if we haven't learned new patterns of eating. Only if our whole response toward food is different can the weight loss be maintained. That is a rather presumptuous statement, and nobody claims it's easy to bring about. And yet, interestingly enough, a behavioral weight-loss program can be less painful to stick to than many other methods, simply because the overeater learns how to remove temptation before it becomes too strong to resist. The basic objective of this kind of program is to alter the environmental conditions associated with eating and exercise, thereby making a permanent change in the ratio of calories consumed to calories expended—with the result, presumably, that the loss of all that flab will also be permanent. And even if there is not an excessive amount of flab to be gotten rid of, this objective is something that most people could do well to keep in mind. After all, there are very few of us who wouldn't be happier if we were to lose five pounds or so, and a behavioral program can be just as effective for people with a minor weight problem as for those who need to lose fifty pounds or more.

Richard Stuart and Barbara Davis have put together one of the most comprehensive behavioral weight-loss programs in their book, *Slim Chance in a Fat World*. A detailed examination of their program will demonstrate why behavioral methods are so effective in dealing with this particular problem.

The general procedure that Stuart and Davis outline consists of pinpointing the environmental conditions—times, places, situations—associated with eating, and then devising ways to alter these conditions. Therefore, as with most behavior-modification procedures, the first step is careful observation, to determine when and where one eats and what happens before and after the overeating. This task is not as easy or as simple-minded as one would imagine. People who overeat are often unaware of how much or how often they eat; suddenly they discover that they are nibbling on something. At this stage a therapist might help his client identify those situations that trigger his overeating or that have been found to encourage others to overeat.

But since a therapist cannot follow his patients around all day, the fat person himself has to do the work. He must be alert and compulsively detailed; it helps to ask himself questions about exactly where and when the eating happens. Do you eat while you're watching TV? While you're talking on the phone? While you're reading? Do you eat mostly in the kitchen or the dining room, or do you wander around the house during your cookie orgies, leaving a trail of crumbs behind? What do you find yourself doing at a party when you're surrounded by aggressive conversationalists and tiny meatballs? How do you end up spending the time when you're depressed and faced with a long, lonely evening to kill?

Plenty of other environmental conditions are often even more insidious than those. Mothers, for example. After all, she only made that special four-layer fudge cake because she loves you. It would be cruel not to devour a hefty piece or two or three (the more the better as far as she's concerned!) after all the trouble she went to. Similarly, you don't want to hurt your hostess at dinner by not plunging into her truffled-stuffed goose and soufflé Grand Marnier. Even at home, how can you expect your slender mate to do without her nightly brownies and milk —even though you always end up eating three times as much as she does? As the research has shown, mostly the overweight person eats not because he's hungry at all but because cues in the environment signal "food."

So now that we have some idea of why we overeat, what do we do about it? What the behavior modifier suggests is that we avoid or alter those "dangerous" situations that encourage our overeating. We must reduce the number of stimuli that signal "food." Essentially we are taking the control of eating away from the situation and the environment, and claiming it for ourselves.

Stuart and Davis suggest that you start by *limiting the number of places in which you eat*. The point is not to go cold turkey and stop eating; it is merely to set aside one place in which you do *all* your eating. Thus, rather than enjoying the midnight snack curled up with a book or in front of the TV set, you go to the dining-room table to have it. And while you're eating you don't do anything else; you don't read or watch TV or talk on the phone—you just eat. The object of this step is to limit the situational cues that suggest food and thereby cause you to eat. If you never eat while reading, then after a while reading won't make you think of food. This step also makes it just plain inconvenient to eat much of the time. If you're watching TV or reading in bed, you're going to be less likely to gobble up a lot of cookies if you have to interrupt your activities by going to the dining-room table to eat.

Unlike in most traditional techniques, the goal of this exercise is the development of new patterns, or habits, of eating, rather than the abrupt reduction of the amount of food consumed. You may at first gorge yourself silly in the dining room, but at least you will be weakening the strong situational control exerted by the TV set. As you carry out this step, you gradually reduce the number of stimuli in the environment signaling "food."

Another important feature of this self-control program is the reduction in the consumption of especially fattening foods. It is an unfortunate coincidence that more often than not, the most fattening foods happen to be the very ones that are shoved down our throats by the media—high-profit fast foods like doughnuts and ice cream and starchy, greasy snacks in endless gimmicky shapes. With gorgeous photography, TV commercials and advertising copy, the food industry modifies our behavior and cleverly evokes from us the response of buying these unnecessary, unhealthy products—and ending up fat.

So how do we fight them? We look at the situation logically and try to figure out how to make it easiest to resist temptation and *as difficult as possible* to succumb to these problem foods. Obviously, if there's a half-gallon of ice cream in your freezer when you suddenly get hungry late at night, you're going to be more likely to eat than if the ice cream isn't there at all. Of course, you can make sure the ice cream isn't going to be there by not buying it in the first place—in other words, by changing your shopping behavior.

The behavior modifier's object here is to teach us ways to reduce the environmental and motivational factors that encourage our indulgence. Essentially the strategy involves removing the temptation before it exists, or before it becomes really strong. In the supermarket, the ice cream seems more remote from us than when it's sitting in the freezer or on the dining-room table, and it is therefore in the shopping situation that we are more likely to resist it. Given these facts of life, much of the program is devoted to developing new shopping habits.

There are several effective ways for us to resist the call of all that seductive garbage on the supermarket shelves. Studies demonstrate that if we shop just after we've eaten, we are a lot less likely to lose control in the bakery aisle than if we haven't eaten for hours and are ravenously hungry. We should plan to shop, therefore, when our stomach is full—then that box of doughnuts just might remain in the store where it belongs, instead of on our shelf and then inevitably in our gullet.

Stuart and Davis also suggest shopping from a list, and only bringing enough money to buy what is on the list. If we try sticking to a list, it's going to be a bit easier to pass up the problem foods that aren't on it. And if we do break down and buy something we shouldn't, that list is going to be there as a tangible reminder that we've transgressed—an aversive consequence we will want to avoid. Although it is time-consuming and rather complicated to compute exactly how much everything we need will cost, the advantages of bringing only the right amount of money are great enough to be well worth the trouble.

Of course it is a rare shopper who is buying food only for himself. Perhaps *herself* would be a more appropriate pronoun, for we must now consider the dilemma of the devoted but overweight mother whose emaciated teen-age sons will make her life hell unless there are gallons of ice-cold Coke on hand for them to swill and three flavors of ice cream for them to devour, at all hours of the day or night. If she's lucky, she herself may not be vulnerable to the foods they demand, but in most cases she is; and in any event, no matter what her tastes, if she's in an eating mood and anything of that sort is around, she'll eat it. And about the only thing the behavior modifier can suggest for her, in terms of shopping, is to try to determine as accurately as possible just how much of the junk her kids consume every day and be sure to buy only that much. That way, if she does eat some of it, there won't be enough for them; and when they open the refrigerator and find that there's no more Coke and only a spoonful of ice cream, they will most likely provide her with some pretty aversive consequences themselves.

Eating between meals is another bad habit that behaviorists believe we must control in order to lose weight and keep it off. One way to help ourselves avoid between-meal eating is to *eat three meals a day*. Too many people skip breakfast or lunch (which usually involve less fattening foods) in an effort to lose weight, and then end up stuffing themselves at dinner and on more fattening snacks in the evening to satisfy the gigantic hunger they have created. If one eats a decent breakfast and lunch, then it will be easier for him not to overindulge at dinner or during the dangerous evening hours.

Stuart and Davis suggest that if we do have to snack, then we should do it, as we've said, in only one room and with less fattening foods. If all we've got to eat as a snack is raw carrots (instead of cookies or potato chips), then we'll be ingesting a lot fewer calories. We may not particularly relish raw carrots, but that's all to the good because then we probably won't feel like snacking so much and eventually may give it up altogether.

So far we've described how to make it more difficult to eat when, where and what we shouldn't. We have outlined ways that have been discovered to limit the environmental stimuli which contribute to our overeating, and set up aversive consequences that result from buying and eating the wrong foods. But behaviorists also have methods for reinforcing the desired eating behavior by helping to make it a little more satisfying than it usually is—as well as more pleasant and a bit easier to cut down on what we eat.

Stuart and Davis recommend using smaller plates and dishes. Four ounces of lean meat and one-half cup of mashed potatoes is going to seem like more than it is when served on a luncheon plate (especially if whoever cooked the meal has been careful to make only enough for one helping, so one is not faced—either at the table or later on—with enticing leftovers).

Another way to make it more likely that we'll eat less is to eat more slowly. It is a well-known physiological fact that the sensation of satiation is delayed. The feeling of a full stomach does not reach the brain until well after the food has reached the stomach. This means that the faster a person eats, the more he will shovel down between the time he really is full and the time he becomes aware of it. If eating can be slowed down, therefore, there will be less food in the stomach when the feeling of fullness finally comes and the person stops eating.

But just telling a person to eat more slowly doesn't help much. In true behavioral fashion, the eating behavior must be observed and specific responses measured. Mouthfuls per minute, for instance. These can easily be recorded, using nothing more than a wristwatch, or a simple supermarket expense counter. Once we know exactly how many times per minute that fork travels from plate to mouth, we'll be better equipped to slow it down—simply because we'll be able to *tell* when we're slowing it down, and when we're not. In addition, we'll be automatically reinforced when we do slow down and punished when we don't, just by knowing whether we're doing better or worse.

Another behavioral procedure is to make sure that each mouthful of food is swallowed before more food is put into the mouth. We can help ourselves stick to this pattern by laying down the knife and fork every time we take a bite and not picking them up again until the food goes down our throat. It's also helpful to eat everything with a knife and fork. A chicken drumstick, a tuna sandwich—all will take longer to eat if we don't eat them with our hands. It's like Westerners eating Chinese food with chopsticks instead of a knife and fork. Chopsticks are harder for most of us to use, eating takes longer —and interestingly enough, Stuart and Davis report that a study has shown that fat people rarely use them.

Finally, in terms of slowing the pace of eating, they suggest interposing a delay shortly after the beginning of the meal, and at several points after that. Just stop eating. Lay down the knife and fork and don't pick them up until a predetermined period of time—two or three minutes—has elapsed. This process may be more difficult than some of the others, but its benefits are very important, for not only will it slow the eating, but once again it will give us the satisfaction of having *control* over what in the past has seemed to be *un*controllable. Labeling our eating as "compulsive," as many people do, simply turns the responsibility for it away from ourselves. All these methods make it easier for us to assume the responsibility and then live up to it successfully.

Nevertheless, these techniques are often still not enough. Behaviorists realize this and have suggested ways of getting help. They recommend that the overeater modify his own social environment as well so that it will reinforce the new self-control behaviors and help him extinguish his own indulgence. This means getting the assistance of family and friends, most of whom (Coke-swilling teen-agers excluded) will be eager to help him get thin. Most practitioners suggest that the person discuss the program with his family or friends and together devise ways that they might help. The wife might be asked not to bake the special dessert but instead prepare the husband's favorite roast. The husband might agree to take his wife out to a special event or buy her a new dress after she has successfully followed the program for a certain period of time. Families have also written contracts in which they promise certain rewards and privileges contingent upon the development of certain new eating habits by the obese person. In all these situations the person who wants to lose weight takes the initiative and directs the program. The program should never be imposed on the person by the family or therapist. If they try against the person's wishes, it will surely fail.

But most families are already likely to be trying to help in this way; they are giving praise and approval when the fat person loses weight, and expressing disappointment when he doesn't. Isn't that enough? Actually, if that *is* what they're doing, they may well be doing him more harm than good. Research in this area has found that it may be a mistake to reinforce someone only for pounds lost. Even a person sticking religiously to the strictest of low-low calorie diets will lose weight erratically. He may lose three pounds in one week and then not lose anything for the next two, even though his caloric intake remains exactly the same. Unfortunately, that just happens to be the way the body works. But imagine how he's going to feel going through those two agonizing weeks and not getting any reinforcement at all—in fact, probably even getting some punishment for *not* losing weight—when he is doing the best he can. Obviously, he's going to feel rotten, he's going to feel helpless, and he may very well decide the whole thing is futile and return to his old eating habits.

So what is necessary if reinforcement for losing weight is not right? When we remember that the goal of a behavioral weight-loss program is to permanently alter the person's eating behavior and not merely to alter his present weight, it becomes clear that he must be reinforced for *how he eats*, not for how much he weighs. After all, he'll be reinforced automatically every time he loses a few pounds, anyway. The point is to help him through the periods when he's following the program but not losing, by telling him what magnificent will power he must have to restrict his eating to the kitchen; by joking with him at the table when he's sitting there with teeth clenched, trying not to pick up his knife and fork; by helping him to figure out how much each item on the shopping list is going to cost, and so on.

Another aspect of the fat person's social environment is the big-wide world outside. When you think about the massive pressure that is put on everyone in this society to be thin—nay, even wraithlike—the effectiveness of all these little personal gambits seems to pale in comparison. Overweight people are painfully discriminated against in almost every way you can think of. They are less likely to be accepted at universities, to be hired by employers or to achieve success in their careers. Socially, of course, they are constantly rejected. And every magazine, movie or TV show they see reminds them of how people are supposed to look, and of what a freak they are. If all that weren't enough to keep a person from being fat, then how can the little bit his friends are able to do have any effect on him?

We've already answered this question. Society's treatment of fat people falls into the category of punishment. In effect, what society does to the fat person is to stimulate him to overeat, with lovely food advertisements and easily accessible fried-chicken and ice-cream franchise restaurants, and then to turn right around and punish him for the results of his overeating! And rather than help him to stop, the punishment usually only makes him miserable and often drives him to eat even more.

What we've been talking about so far are the methods that are more or less unique to a behavioral weight-loss program: *how to permanently change our eating habits.* Behaviorists of course recognize the importance of devising a sensible diet. In this area they turn to nutrition and diet experts to set up a diet in which the amount of calories taken in is balanced with the amount used up through exercise while at the same time maintaining high quality nutrition.

But in the area of exercise the behaviorist still has more to add. It's very easy to tell a person to get enough exercise to balance his caloric intake but not so easy to do. For most people, and especially fat people, exercise, in the words of Stuart and Davis, "is not a richly reinforcing experience." What the behaviorists have offered are ways to make it easier and thereby more likely that we'll burn up excess calories. Once again, it's a question of situational control, of establishing the antecedents and consequences of exercise (and nonexercise), and then altering them to make the desired behavior more likely to occur. To eliminate the antecedents of nonexercise, one might remove the snack tray and the mini-refrigerator from the TV room so that eating requires a brisk hike to the kitchen. Or tape up the clothes chute so that you have to carry the dirty clothes to the basement. Lock the door on the downstairs bathroom, and so on.

The behaviorists suggest that one way to strengthen the antecedents of exercise is to provide companionship so that it becomes a social event—and that does *not* mean setting up a ruggedly competitive football game with lots of lean athletic types, which would probably do a marvelous job of turning the overweight person away from exercise forever. Instead, go for walks. You can talk, look at interesting scenery or neighborhoods, even bring along a radio and listen to the game (instead of observing it with a six-pack in a lounge chair in front of the TV). Starting out with a gentle overall exercise like walking will also eliminate the aversive consequences of sore muscles and fatigue that can result from sudden and unaccustomed strenuous exercise. *After* the body has gradually adjusted to more exercise is the time to arrange for more strenuous activity with others, either with friends or by going to a nearby gym.

At the beginning it is also important to provide positive consequences. Praise, of course, is effective, but perhaps more tangible evidence of approval such as gifts should also be offered. Here, too, contingency contracts may be set up so that, for example, the overweight person will be able to watch his favorite TV show only if he goes on his twenty-minute walk beforehand. But eventually these prodding techniques may not even be necessary. Though it may be difficult for the inactive person to believe, the results of exercise are so gratifying it may eventually be as sorely missed as it was once detested. An interesting positive side effect of increased exercise is a natural reduction in the amount of food consumed. Research has shown that increases in general amount of physical activity lead to a reduction, not an increase, in eating. Thus the exercise program has a double-barreled effect: it burns up calories and reduces our intake of food.

To help keep up this balance between caloric intake and output, the behaviorist would also suggest making charts and graphs of *eating and exercise behavior* (*not* just graphs of pounds lost). A comparison of the two will show the dieter exactly what is happening at any point. In this way one can learn how his own particular metabolism works in relation to caloric intake and output, correct mistakes he might be making, and then be reinforced by the graph for doing well.

But to make such a graph requires a knowledge of nutrition—to be able to make any decision *at all* about how one is going to eat requires a knowledge of nutrition. It's all very well to be handed a day-by-day schedule of everything you're supposed to eat for the next month, but at some point during that time you will doubtless find yourself in an unexpected situation in which you will have to decide for yourself. And in order to decide what to do to maintain a balance, it will be necessary to understand the body's way of using calories. Therefore an important step in any program is education.

Though the intensely rewarding results of the new eating behavior are a powerful reinforcement for sticking to the system, often they are not reinforcement enough, and people do tend to drop out. However, once again the behaviorist can reach into his bag of tricks and come up with ways to make staying in the program a little easier and dropping out harder. For instance, the overweight person can hand over to the practitioner who is guiding his program a substantial amount of money which he earns back for staying in the program. As he maintains the new eating and exercise habits, the money is periodically paid back to him in small amounts. If he drops out, his money is forfeited to the politician he dislikes most. Thus, he's paying himself for staying in the program.

This all sounds extremely reasonable. But how about proof? Has anybody actually shown that a program like this works better than anything else?

As a matter of fact, they have. As we indicated earlier in

this chapter, numerous research studies have compared the effectiveness of behavioral weight-loss programs with psychotherapeutic and medical programs, and the results have shown consistently that most people on a behavioral program, even when the program is administered only by a manual and there is no contact with a therapist at all, lose more weight faster and keep it off longer than people in the other programs. Although it is true that we lack long-term follow-up data, it seems, from where we stand now, that these techniques are extremely promising.

We have spent an inordinate amount of time on overeating, but then, overeating is an inordinate problem in this culture, and the behavioral strategies for dealing with it are especially clear examples of self-control procedures. But how about other self-inflicted problems that are difficult to control? How about smoking?

Smoking does seem to be similar to overeating in that it shares that deceitful characteristic of being immediately pleasurable and then leading to long-term negative consequences (and we all know what those negative consequences are). Also, like overeating, most people have a hell of a time trying to give it up. So is anything being done?

Scientists have tried all sorts of things to get people to stop smoking. People have been placed in an apparatus that blew an unpleasant mixture of smoke and hot air into their faces while they were smoking, and a refreshing blast of fresh air when they put out the cigarette. Subjects were seated in a booth to listen to music, but each time they drew on the cigarette, unpleasant static interrupted the music. These methods have all been notably without success, and the reason seems clear: the smoker does not live in the laboratory, and no matter what happens there, most of the time he is going to be on his own and free to smoke as much as he wants.

As with overeating, the only person who really has any power to stop someone from smoking is the smoker himself because he is the only one who's around every time he wants a cigarette. Techniques of self-control, then, seem to be the most promising answer. At the risk of being repetitious, we should explain how therapists have applied these techniques.

The program begins with determining the antecedents and consequences of smoking, then altering the antecedents, reducing the positive consequences and increasing the negative consequences. To a certain extent this technique has even been used on a nationwide level. Though the people who brought the programs about probably wouldn't have described them in these words, altering the antecedents and consequences was exactly what was done when cigarette ads were removed from television and warnings put on cigarettes packages—not to mention all those gruesome antismoking campaigns showing diseased lungs. The theory was that if the ads were taken away, people wouldn't be influenced, and reminded, to smoke; and that putting the warning on the cigarette package would make the consequences of reaching for a cigarette more unpleasant. These are worthwhile measures; certainly the mass media have done a lot more to help smokers than they ever did for fat people. Yet, in the face of all these good intentions, it has not worked. In fact, since these campaigns began there has been an actual *increase* in the frequency of smoking. Many behaviorists claim that this failure did not surprised them. They argue that the mistake was in making the programs too general. After all, there are plenty of things a lot more immediate than TV commercials that make people want a cigarette; just getting rid of the commercials won't do the trick (though it's still a good idea, of course). As for the negative consequences, you can always turn off the TV when one of those depressing antismoking messages comes on, and who spends a lot of time reading cigarette packages, anyway? No; as with overeating, the answer must lie in more individualized applications of self-control procedures.

So the practitioner can start by asking an individual smoker what environmental events make him want a cigarette, in order to determine which environmental events to alter or avoid. And he will say, "Well, I've got to have one with my first cup of coffee in the morning, and another after I've eaten breakfast, and while I'm in the car driving to work I need a couple, and then I want one right after I get to the office, where everybody else is smoking, and then while I'm working I've got to have cigarettes and coffee to keep me going, I couldn't work without them, and then with a drink before lunch, to relax, and then after lunch, of course, and all afternoon I—"

Hold it! Something is wrong here. *Everything* makes him want a cigarette, so how can he avoid, or even alter, everything? And here we find ourselves faced with one of the differences between smoking and overeating. The stimuli in the environment that signal smoking are far greater than those associated with food. Seeing a photograph of a cake or driving past a fried-chicken place may make you want to eat, but it is certainly easier to avoid those situations than it is to avoid your morning cup of coffee, breakfast, the drive to work, the office itself, and so on through the day. In fact, there are few situations in which you can't smoke—if you think about it, you may come up with two or three—but there are plenty of places where eating is impossible. Most people cannot, therefore, avoid or alter the antecedents of smoking. Does that mean that behavior modifiers are helpless in trying to establish self-control?

Not quite. Just as they did with the fat person who ate all day in every room of the house, they have tried to help the smoker restrict the times and/or places in which smoking occurs, in the hope of limiting the situational cues that signal smoking. The smoker will find it a lot easier to modify his environment if there is only *one* situation that makes him smoke, and not twenty.

Toward this end, many clever methods have been devised. One way of establishing situational control is quite similar to a method we described in relation to overeating. A "smoking place" is established, one particular chair, for instance; the smoker can smoke only in that chair, and while he is smoking he must not do anything but smoke—he can't read or watch TV or talk to anyone, and the people he lives with must be instructed not to talk to him then, either. Supposedly the smoker will get tired of turning off the TV or turning off his mouth, and racing to the chair every time he wants a cigarette, and will therefore smoke less. To increase this effect he can eventually move the chair to the basement. In the end the whole situation will become too silly and inconvenient for the smoker to take, the theory goes, and he'll give up cigarettes.

Another method involves the use of a special cigarette case. This charming tool has a time lock built into it so that it will open and offer the smoker one cigarette only after a certain interval. It starts out easy, but as time goes on it opens less and less, until finally it does not open at all. But why, you may be asking, doesn't he just go out and buy a new pack of cigarettes and ignore the damn thing? And that happens to be exactly what Soviet Premier Leonid Brezhnev did when he tried to curb his smoking with just such a device. He confessed to the press, "I have a reserve pack in the other pocket."

In fact, all the methods we have covered are just about that successful. We might as well admit right now that with smoking, *nothing* works very well, neither behavior modification, nor group therapy, nor most smoking clinics—with one notable and encouraging exception, which we will get to in a minute. For the most part, however, all methods fail to just about the same degree: only 5 percent of the people who begin these programs successfully give up the habit for as long as six months.

But why is it so difficult? What is there about smoking that makes it so much harder to control than other unwanted behaviors? There are many answers. The desire for a cigarette is so powerful in most smokers that it is difficult to come up with any method powerful enough, short of torture, to compete with it. Not that the environment doesn't sometimes come up with a powerful enough stimulus: one's husband dying of lung cancer, for instance; one's house burning down because of smoking in bed; having a heart attack. But these catastrophies do not always happen, and furthermore, they don't necessarily result in a person's quitting. Just think of that famous lady who had her larynx removed because of cancer and went right on smoking through the hole in her throat.

For most people, unfortunately, the negative consequences of smoking are too remote and not probable enough —certainly less so than the consequences associated with overeating. If you ingest more calories than you use up, it won't be long before you'll be fat, period, no matter who you are. Lung cancer, on the other hand, takes years to develop, and plenty of smokers never get it at all. We all know people who have smoked for fifty years and are perfectly healthy. It's the most human of all responses to think of oneself as special, that "it won't happen to me," and thereby ignore the ultimate aversive consequences of smoking. But it's not so easy to ignore weighing 350 pounds.

Another problem is the one we mentioned earlier, that there are so many situations in which people smoke that it's almost impossible even to isolate them, let alone change or avoid them. Furthermore, there is much controversy over whether smoking is just a nasty habit or a real addiction—and if it is an addiction, then there are physical as well as behavioral factors involved. Finally, there is really no incompatible response to smoking—in other words, no substitute. If you need to eat, you can stuff yourself with carrots instead of candy bars (not really a *great* substitute, but a substitute nonetheless), but when you need a cigarette, you need a cigarette, and nothing else will do.

There is, however, one program—the exception we mentioned earlier—that has been somewhat more successful than all the rest. Working with volunteers at Northwestern University's Quit Smoking Clinic, psychologist Judith Flaxman discovered that establishing a specific date at which the smoker abruptly stops—he just goes cold turkey—can improve the effectiveness of the self-control techniques. Her method begins with a two-week training program in which she not only teaches the smoker all the self-control techniques outlined earlier but also gives him the usual antismoking propaganda. During this period he is encouraged to prepare himself to quit and is instructed to announce to all his friends that this time he is really going to stop—so that the embarrassment he'll have to face if he starts again will be an immediate aversive consequence. In a carefully designed research study, she compared this method with others and found it to be by far the most effective. At the end of six months, 50 percent of those who followed the abrupt-quitting, self-control method were still not smoking—and that is clearly superior to the 5 percent success rate we cited earlier.

Still, 50 percent is only half, and *all* the people in the program must have been really motivated to stop (after all, they entered the program voluntarily in the first place), so obviously there is still a long way to go.

But—we have yet to mention one important, and perhaps hopeful, aspect of the smoking question: there *are* people who just stop smoking. On their own, without going to clinics or using clever little machines or experiencing disasters in their lives, they stop. Awe-inspiring or infuriating though they may be, they are, in any case, the harbingers of hope in this generally grim picture.

Unfortunately, behavior modifiers as well as medical authorities cannot fully explain why these ex-smokers succeed. It may have to do with their particular personality types; it may, as Flaxman suggests, depend to some extent on stopping abruptly rather than gradually easing off. But it is something that works. Research, behavioral and otherwise, on smoking continues and one promising avenue might be to make carefully detailed studies of those who are able to stop.

Though the specific techniques we've been describing are relatively new, it is not exactly a new idea to talk about using self-control to combat activities like smoking and overeating. After all, we are the ones who are doing these things to ourselves, so self-control seems the obvious way to try to stop. And it would be natural to assume that the use of self-control techniques would be limited to similar, consciously carried out behaviors, such as spending too much money or nagging at your spouse—things that you know you really *should* try to control and perhaps chastise yourself for not controlling.

But psychologists are now developing self-control techniques that allow the individual to regulate less obviously self-controllable problems—important bodily functions—such as blood pressure and brain waves. Of course, vast theoretical implications leap from this radical concept of man's developing control over visceral functions that he has always presumed to be totally involuntary. But it is the practical, medical implications that concern us here. These techniques offer the possibility of the relief, through self-control, of such serious conditions as hypertension, migraine headaches and epileptic seizures.

The study of visceral learning has only just begun, and as of yet sufficient follow-up data have not been amassed to allow sweeping claims about what it can and cannot do; nevertheless, the results that have been achieved so far are upsetting certain beliefs that Western man has held for centuries.

A new, highly technical procedure called biofeedback makes these results possible. It is intended to make the individual aware of specific bodily functions of which he is not normally aware—by electronically adding new senses to the five old standards all healthy human beings possess. Because we can see where we are going, we can avoid bumping into things; it is our eyes that give us control. We cannot control certain functions such as blood pressure and brain waves because we cannot monitor them; we cannot "feel" them. But by means of electronic equipment that records physiological responses and then feeds back the information to the individual, he can be taught to regulate these functions. Through biofeedback he can "feel" his blood pressure. An apt analogy would be that of a blindfolded baseball player trying to hit a curve ball. Biofeedback takes off the blindfold.

The way that an individual is taught to control these functions is really quite simple, although the mechanisms involved are puzzling. The procedure begins by his being rewarded for any desired change in the readings on the physiological monitor. If, for example, he suffers from high blood pressure, he might receive a penny or hear a few seconds of pleasant music each time his recorded blood pressure goes below its usual level. In some cases just seeing the needle on the dial show a decline is reinforcement enough. And even though our hypertensive patient often cannot identify exactly what he is *doing* to make the responses change, nevertheless immediate reinforcement for such changes results in his being able to control them.

Still, even with the use of these gadgets, the idea that the conscious mind can have any control over the internal organs seems far-fetched to most of us. This is not true in other cultures. For centuries, practitioners of rajas and hatha yoga have successfully exerted self-control over these same internal functions, without the use of any equipment at all. Most Western scientists considered these disciplines irrelevant, if not bogus, until their own electronic gadgetry began to tell them that there might be something to them. Now scientists are learning a great deal by studying yoga and Zen practitioners, and what they are learning indicates that conscious control of internal functions is indeed physically possible. For the yogi it requires a lifetime of discipline, study and a special attitude toward the universe; modern psychology does it with machines.

Their goals, of course, are not the same. To the yogi, the physical control is the side issue, a pathway to another state of consciousness. The goal of the researchers is to learn how to establish the physical control and then put it to clinical use.

We can get a clearer picture of what all this means by describing some actual research. Harvard University professors Gary Schwarts and David Shapiro set out to teach healthy college students to raise and lower their blood pressure. This research would have been impossible without new and specially developed equipment that measured blood pressure after each heartbeat and instantly relayed the information to the subject in the form, for example, of a red light indicating that the pressure had gone up, a green light indicating that it had gone down. In order to make sure that the students would not try to change their blood pressure by hyperventilating, all they were told was to keep the light blinking either red or green, and that after a certain number of correct responses they would be rewarded by being shown an interesting picture on the screen.

Amazingly enough, it worked. Those who were reinforced for raising their blood pressure kept it up, those who were reinforced for lowering it kept it down. And they were not doing it by trying to slow down their whole system in general, or speed up the system—no change occurred in either heart rate or muscle tension when the students successfully controlled their blood pressure. The *only* response that changed was the specific one that was being reinforced, the blood pressure itself. These exciting results suggest that people with chronic hypertension may be able to learn to lower their own blood pressure, without using drugs.

Then why isn't every person suffering from hypertension given this self-control training? In some clinics it is actually being used on an experimental basis. But more work needs to be done both to improve the techniques and to make absolutely sure that there really are no long-term side effects before the procedure can be put into general use. And there is another problem. People can lower their blood pressure just fine when they're in the laboratory and hooked up to the biofeedback machine, but as soon as they take off the machine, that "blindfold" goes on again. That is, since they can no longer tell when their blood pressure needs to go down, they lose control over it. It's nice for a person to be able to go in for an appointment and lower his blood pressure, but what is really needed is some way to let him lower it any time and anywhere. With increased technology, one can imagine a device that a person could wear like a wristwatch which would let him know, with a red light perhaps, when his blood pressure was going up, so that he could then lower it before it reached the danger point. Research seems to indicate that such a device would work; we just don't know how to make it. And that means that self-control of high blood pressure is still stuck in the laboratory.

But self-control of certain other maladies—migraine headaches, for instance—is not. The agony of migraine is legendary, and the drugs used to treat it are frequently not very effective and full of unpleasant side effects. But now researchers at the Menninger Foundation in Topeka, Kansas, are exploring a method for training migraine sufferers to gain control of their headaches without using drugs.

The work is that of psychologists Elmer Green and Dale Waters and internist Joseph Sargent. Their project began as a study of what is known as *autogenic feedback training.* In the early 1900's a German psychiatrist, Johannes Schultz, developed a self-hypnotic therapeutic technique which he labeled autogenic training. The patient repeated certain phrases to himself over and over again, such as "I am beginning to feel relaxed, I am getting more and more relaxed . . . My body feels heavier and heavier . . ." until he achieved a relaxed state that was the direct opposite of stress, and eliminating stress eliminates many psychosomatic disorders. The Menninger scientists were trying to combine autogenic training with biofeedback in an effort to help people with circulatory ailments control the flow of blood in their arteries. They knew that when an especially large amount of blood flowed through the hands, the temperature of the hands would rise. And so they hooked up the volunteer subjects to a machine that measured the temperature of their hands, and had them repeat autogenic phrases like "I feel relaxed . . . My arms and hands are heavy and warm . . . Warmth is flowing into my hands . . ." in the hope that they would learn to move quantities of blood into their hands at will.

One of the subjects, who suffered from migraine headaches, happened to have an attack during one of the early training sessions. To make her as comfortable as possible they let her sit in a quiet, dark room, but they did not unhook the measuring device from her hands. In a few minutes the temperature in her hands suddenly rose ten degrees and at that precise moment her headache disappeared.

This unexpected event turned out to make a lot of sense. Since excessive blood flow in the scalp accompanies a migraine headache, the scientists reasoned that if a patient could get the blood out of his scalp and into his hands, the headache would go away. They therefore set about to train a group of people with migraines to learn to control the flow of blood in their hands by having them concentrate on the autogenic phrases while at the same time receiving feedback about the temperature of their hands.

They also went one step further and instructed the subjects to practice at home. If they could be weaned away from the biofeedback machine, if they could learn to "feel" the blood in their hands with no outside help, then they might learn to control or even prevent their headaches themselves, any time and anywhere.

Sixty-three percent of the subjects did learn. At the first sign of a headache they would repeat to themselves the autogenic phrases and concentrate on feeling warmth in their hands. And the headache would go away. One woman learned so well that the process eventually became nearly automatic; all she had to do was give a mental command to the headache to "Go away!" and the headache would obediently depart.

One important aspect of this work is that people with migraines can be more easily weaned away from the dependence on biofeedback equipment because their treatment involves a physical sensation— warmth in their hands—that they can really learn to feel, whereas hypertense people cannot feel their blood pressure go up and must always depend on equipment to tell them when it does.

But the most fantastic application of biofeedback is the self-control of brain waves. At this point we know very little about these most elusive of bodily functions, and one may very well question the necessity of controlling them at all. All we can do for an answer is to give examples of what is being done.

By now everyone probably knows something about meditation, the practice of spending certain specific periods of time every day sitting quietly away from any noise and distraction, trying to think about nothing—to empty, and in a sense "cleanse," the mind, to get rid of all the drivel that pours through our heads most of the time. For many people, meditation really seems to work. They achieve in meditation a pleasurable state of alert and creative calmness that does have a beneficial effect on them, even when they are not meditating.

Whenever a person is in this state of meditation his brain emits waves of a particular frequency and wavelength known as alpha waves. As with hypertension, people cannot feel their own brain waves, but machines can measure them and the information can be fed back to the individual. The results are still far from conclusive, but there is evidence that with biofeedback some people can learn to control alpha waves and achieve the pleasurable state associated with them.

But there are other brain waves, much more specific than alpha. Psychologist Maurice B. Sterman of the Veterans Administration Hospital in West Los Angeles, California, and his associates have isolated a brain-wave pattern emitted by the sensorimotor cortex, which is the part of the brain that controls the muscles. This particular pattern, which they call the *sensorimotor rhythm* (SMR), is associated with muscular relaxation. It is emitted, in other words, when the muscles are *not* moving. In an experiment with cats, they fed the animals only when they were emitting SMR; as a result the cats learned to stand as still as statues when they wanted to be fed. Going further, Sterman reasoned that if epileptics, whose skeletal muscles go uncontrollably wild during a seizure, could be trained to emit SMR, they might gain at least some control over their seizures. Four preliminary subjects were given biofeedback training along the same lines we've described in other studies; they were rewarded when their SMR level went up. They did learn to increase their SMR in the laboratory and as a result the frequency of their seizures *outside* the laboratory dropped as well. One six-year-old boy who had been having as many as twenty-five seizures a week was free of seizures after only six months of training.

Although there is a marked reduction in the frequency of seizures outside the laboratory while the patient is receiving biofeedback training, it also appears that when training is finally terminated, the frequency of seizures again increases. In order to correct this problem Dr. Sterman and his associates are now investigating the possibility of patients using a biofeed-back machine at home so that they can practice the training on a daily or weekly basis. With regular practice the patient may maintain the reduction in the frequency of seizures.

Of course it would benefit us greatly to know exactly what the person does when he successfully controls these bodily functions, but at this time no one really understands how it happens. Much of the current research in the area of biofeed-back is directed toward this question. All that is known is that by receiving reinforcement for changes in these functions, people become able to control them. Those who have mastered this self-control have offered many hypotheses, but none of them has been proven.

This kind of self-control is far removed from the methods for losing weight we discussed at the beginning of this chapter. But although the details and the technology differ, the underly-ing principle of altering the environment so that one is rein-forced for emitting the desired behavior is basically the same. That concept is the root of the behavioral approach to self-control. We said it isn't magic, and clearly it is not. It is quite possible that the experts may *never* figure out a foolproof way to stop smoking. Nevertheless, applying those simple learning principles to ourselves does seem to have a real effect on our behavior.

VI
Anxiety

We are living, as W. H. Auden put it, in the Age of Anxiety. No mere poetic metaphor, his words are indeed a statement of fact, to which the vast and ever increasing sales of Librium, Valium and numerous other tranquilizers stand as an undeniable testament.

Not that anxiety is necessarily all bad. It is a physiological response that was built into our nervous system for a reason. Increased alertness, fast thinking and a quickened metabolism in general are functions of anxiety that enable us to perform better in dangerous or stressful situations. Everyone has heard stories about the ordinarily sluggish matron who makes a record-breaking dash to save an infant from toppling into a swimming pool, or the 97-pound weakling who lifts up the front half of a Mercedes-Benz to rescue a trapped companion. Anxiety is a vital survival mechanism without which we would be far more vulnerable creatures than we already are.

But too much of a good thing can be destructive, and

excessive or inappropriate anxiety certainly takes its toll in many familiar forms. There are the various phobias that can interfere with normal functioning, sometimes to the extent that the sufferer becomes a true cripple. There is insomnia. Impotence and other forms of sexual dysfunction are, in many cases, the result of anxiety. There are also its physiological manifestations, such as ulcers and severe headaches. The psychodynamic approach to these problems has been to attempt to uncover some trauma or childhood conflict, often "repressed," which is presumed to be the cause of the anxiety. Behaviorists, not surprisingly, believe that the laborious and time-consuming procedure of trying to unearth some hypothetical cause has little if any therapeutic value. The survivor of a plane crash may understand very well why he is afraid of flying, but that knowledge does not necessarily eradicate the fear. So behaviorists make use of certain specialized techniques to attack disabling anxiety directly, with the goal of just making it go away. And, the popularity of Librium notwithstanding, behaviorists eschew the use of drugs. They train the anxious person to control the anxiety himself, without artificial help.

Anxiety can be divided into three categories. Appropriate and constructive anxiety, as we have seen, is a resource we could not do without. But anxiety can be appropriate and at the same time have destructive effects. A good example would be a policeman working in a tough neighborhood who experiences extremely discomforting anxiety during gunfights with crooks. Though the anxiety may keep him awake at night, it nevertheless makes him better equipped to dodge bullets and take accurate aim, and to tamper with it would be perilous indeed. A behavior therapist, therefore, would not try to eliminate the anxiety, but would instead recommend that the policeman be moved to a different beat or even change jobs.

Finally, there is anxiety that is both destructive and inappropriate, and that frequently results in the problems we mentioned earlier. Unlike the appropriate anxiety experienced by the policeman, inappropriate anxiety, such as an overwhelming fear of elevators, serves no useful function and only causes difficulties for the individual who suffers from it. The behaviorist seeks to eliminate this type of anxiety.

One of the most important tools in the treatment of anxiety is a procedure known as *progressive relaxation training,* first developed in 1934 by Edmund Jacobson at Harvard University. He observed that muscle tension always accompanies anxiety, and that anxiety in fact could not occur when the muscles were relaxed; and he reasoned that if an anxious person could learn to relax his muscles, he would diminish, if not eliminate, his anxiety. It is a physiological fact that a muscle undergoes greater relaxation after it has been contracted, so Jacobson's procedure consisted of systematically tensing and then relaxing various muscle groups until total muscular relaxation was achieved. By carefully going through this procedure, and learning to be aware of the sensation of muscular tension and relaxation, an anxious person can learn to relax. The only problem was that the original method was rather unwieldy, since it took fifty-six training sessions to learn how to do it.

In 1948 psychiatrist Joseph Wolpe modified the method so that the training only required six 20-minute sessions, with two daily 15-minute practice sessions at home. Wolpe also took the procedure one step further by developing a method for pairing the relaxation response with the anxiety-producing stimuli. If a person with a fear of elevators, for example, could learn to concentrate on elevators *while in a state of deep relaxation,* then he would eventually associate elevators with relaxation instead of tension, and would no longer find them a source of anxiety—since anxiety cannot occur when the muscles are relaxed. This final goal, however, must be approached through a series of discrete steps, because just thinking about an elevator is enough to jolt an elevator-phobe out of his relaxed state. The patient and the therapist together make out a list of hierarchies, beginning with the least anxiety-producing situation—approaching a building in which there is an elevator, for instance—and moving very gradually toward the most frightening situation, riding in the elevator itself. Then, once the person has learned how to relax, the therapist asks him to concentrate on the first item on the list. Once he can remain relaxed while concentrating on approaching the building, he is asked to concentrate on the next item—entering the building —and so on, until he is capable of remaining fully relaxed while imagining riding on the elevator itself. An ideal list of hierarchies would approach the final situation so gradually that the client remains relaxed at all times. This process is known as *systematic desensitization,* and to see just how it works we can examine an actual case study reported by Dr. Stanley Rachman.

The client was a young schoolteacher who had a longstanding fear of injections of any kind and would go to great lengths to avoid them. On those few occasions when she could not avoid them, she would faint before the needle was actually inserted. Even talking about the subject upset her. She also reported having certain sexual problems and even had difficulty using tampons.

After lengthy discussion the therapist decided that her primary fear concerned injections and that the sexual problems were secondary. He began by focusing on her fear of injections and of using tampons. With her help they devised a nine-item hierarchy related to tampons. The first item was the mildest, just a box of tampons, but they became more and more disturbing, and the ninth item—walking about with a tampon inserted—was the most disturbing thought of all. After she had become quite skillful at relaxing, the therapist asked her to concentrate on the first items on the list while in a state of relaxation. She gradually moved up the hierarchy as each item became less disturbing, and by the ninth session she felt no anxiety about tampons and was able to insert them quickly, with little or no pain.

Her fear of injections was treated in the same way. A hierarchy was constructed, consisting of (1) seeing a hypodermic syringe, (2) holding a syringe, (3) filling a syringe, (4) seeing a slide of a person receiving an injection, (5) seeing a ball receive an injection, (6) seeing a dog receive an injection, (7) another person being injected, (8) the client herself being injected at home, and (9) the client being injected in a clinic. Over the next five sessions she was asked to concentrate on each item until it caused no discomfort, and then move on to the next. Finally she was given a practice injection while under relaxation, and a week later an ordinary injection at a clinic. On both occasions she was slightly uncomfortable, but did not overreact and showed no signs of fainting.

Her sexual problem involved a fear of penetration combined with pain experienced during intercourse. This problem diminished to some extent after she had overcome her fear of tampons and injections, but more treatment was needed. The therapist had to work on this problem only for a few sessions. With brief desensitization to sexual situations, she showed marked improvement and the therapy was terminated. Five years later she reported that none of the phobias had returned, even though she had been exposed to many stressful situations.

In one of the most rigorously scientific evaluations of a specific psychological treatment, psychologist Gordon L. Paul of the University of Illinois studied the effects of systematic desensitization as compared to other forms of therapy on a group of college students who were terrified of speaking in public. As we have described, the students were first taught to relax, and then a hierarchy was constructed for each individual. Each hierarchy ended with the situation of the client's speaking before a group of people. The students then worked through the hierarchy until they could relax while concentrating on the last item on the list. The treatment was extremely effective: 100 percent of the students who received systematic desensitization improved, as compared to only 73 percent in the most successful alternative treatment. Physiological measures of anxiety, such as heart rate and blood pressure, also showed marked decreases following the treatment program. As Paul put it:

> The findings were overwhelmingly positive, and for the first time in the history of psychological treatments, a specific

treatment package reliably produced measurable benefits for clients across a broad range of distressing problems in which anxiety was of fundamental importance. "Relapse" and "symptom substitution" were notably lacking.[1]

Relaxation training can also work in cases where inappropriate anxiety is not related to one specific fear. Take insomnia, which has plagued almost everyone at some time or another. Once the insomniac learns how to relax in the therapist's office, he practices the technique at home in bed, before going to sleep. And in most cases he falls asleep fast—without resorting to sleeping pills.

One case, reported by Dr. Lester Tobias, involved a female college student who for years had feared fire, the dark and being alone. She could sleep only if the lights were on all night and if someone else was in the room with her. She had always been able to arrange her life so that these requirements were met, but when an opportunity to study abroad occurred, she realized that if she went, the conditions would not be met— she would not be able to sleep and would have to give up the trip. Seven weeks before departure she contacted a behavior therapist. He taught her how to use progressive relaxation and had her practice it at home in bed. He also instructed her to decrease the light in the room a little more each night while she relaxed, and to begin relaxing just a bit earlier every night, to get used to relaxing for longer periods of time before her roommate came home and while she was alone. After several weeks she reported that she was having no trouble getting to sleep and that her fears were greatly reduced.

Insomnia is not the only anxiety-related problem people experience in the bedroom. In their recent book (which provides a particularly lucid discussion of the treatment of sexual inadequacy), Daniel O'Leary and Terrance Wilson quote Masters and Johnson's statement that a "conservative estimate would indicate half the marriages [in this country] as either presently sexual dysfunctional or imminently so in the future."[2] This situation is particularly alarming when we realize that until quite recently, no one really knew what to do about premature ejaculation, impotence in men or frigidity in women. Therapists considered them extremely difficult, if not unsolvable, problems.

Behaviorists believe that these problems are only very rarely related to physical illness or deep-seated psychiatric disorder. Usually they stem from ignorance about sex, lack of opportunity, or dissatisfaction of one kind or another with one's sexual partners. In most cases these factors result in what is known as "performance anxiety," which, in more colloquial terms, means being afraid you aren't going to be able to cut it. It is the fear of not being able to perform that renders one incapable of performing well. Masters and Johnson's treatment consists essentially of education coupled with desensitization to eliminate the fear. By far the most successful treatment for these problems that has yet to come along, it has arrived not a moment too soon, for many authorities believe the "sexual revolution" has increased, rather than decreased, people's sexual anxieties. The pervasive sentiment that there is something wrong with anyone who is not a sexual athlete only makes the consequences of failure all the more devastating—and correspondingly, any "performance anxiety" will be just that much more debilitating.

Masters and Johnson begin by taking a detailed sexual history of the client. From the very beginning, in both the presentation of the questions and the therapists' responses to the client's story, they scrupulously avoid any suggestion that the client is "sexually abnormal." Such an attitude on the part of the therapists would only make him feel more uncomfortable about sex than he already does. He might cover up or lie about certain important details. And he might experience difficulty trusting and confiding in the therapist, which is all-important if the treatment is going to succeed. They also require that both partners in the sexual relationship, or marriage, participate in the treatment, even though only one partner may be clearly dysfunctional. They consider that "the relationship between the partners is the patient." Sexual behavior does not exist in a vacuum; the problem involves both partners, and increased communication and understanding between partners is vital for success. And since therapy involves two partners, there are also two co-therapists, male and female. The use of co-therapists prevents either client from feeling outnumbered by the opposite sex. Furthermore, someone of the same sex who has grown up with similar conditioning will undoubtedly have a deeper understanding of the client's sexual feelings than a member of the opposite sex, and will not only be more likely to inspire confidence in the client but also be better able to communicate specific details.

As with the treatment of phobias, the function of desensitization in sex therapy is to train the client not to respond with anxiety to certain specific stimuli—in this case, the situation of being expected to perform sexually. To start with, the clients are instructed *not* to engage in any sexual acts that the therapist does not specifically permit. Though this rule may at first seem dictatorial on the therapist's part, it is nevertheless one of the most important aspects of the entire treatment. If the client knows that he must not have intercourse with his partner and that all that is permitted is some mutual fondling, then he will not feel performance anxiety because there are in fact no expectations placed upon him to perform. The sexual situation will no longer arouse anxiety, and he can relax and concentrate on enjoying himself and pleasing his partner in other ways, instead of worrying about whether or not he'll be able to complete intercourse. In this atmosphere of relaxation and no expectations, the partners go through a carefully graduated series of sexual exercises. It's "homework," with the goal of increasing mutual comfort, communication and sensual awareness. As anxiety is gradually extinguished and arousal begins to occur on its own, then the exercises become directed toward the specific sexual problem.

Masters and Johnson most frequently encountered one particular combination of problems. Premature ejaculation in the male was coupled with orgasmic dysfunction—the inability to have orgasms, popularly known as "frigidity"—in the female. One can see that these problems belong together.

Though premature ejaculation may not appear to be as debilitating a problem as actual impotence, it nevertheless makes it impossible for a couple to achieve satisfying sexual rapport. The male reaches orgasm so quickly that the female may not even get aroused, let alone experience orgasm herself. The treatment begins, as we have described, with the couple engaging in relaxed sensual exercises with no expectation of performance. Actual penetration is prohibited. Instead, the female manually stimulates the penis almost to the point of orgasm. But just when orgasm is about to occur, she firmly squeezes the penis on either side of the coronal ridge for a few seconds, which prevents ejaculation. Then she begins all over again. In this way the male learns to maintain his erection without ejaculating for increasingly longer periods of time. In the next step the woman straddles the man to insert his penis into her vagina and then just leaves it there, without the usual thrusting motions. After he becomes capable of insertion without ejaculation, they then gradually build up to more and more vigorous thrusting. Whenever ejaculation seems imminent, the woman, who is on top of the man and therefore has a certain control over the situation, removes the penis and repeats the squeeze technique, to prevent ejaculation. The penis is then inserted again. It is not long before they are having intercourse for fifteen minutes and longer without ejaculation. In many cases, women who had never before experienced orgasm reached spontaneous climaxes while practicing the procedure. This treatment was successful in 182 of the 186 cases of premature ejaculation treated by Masters and Johnson.

There are a variety of causes for orgasmic dysfunction in women. Many women have just never had the chance to reach orgasm because their experience has been limited to incompetent or indifferent men who have no skill, or no interest, in arousing them. Anxiety about sex, often a result of religious or parental conditioning, is another common problem. Masters and Johnson consider society's double standard (fortunately now on the wane), which deems it appropriate for men, but not women, to enjoy sex, one of the primary reasons why many women have difficulty achieving orgasm.

Education and counseling are therefore important aspects of the treatment for female orgasmic dysfunction. The counseling is not limited to the woman, however, but also deals with any interpersonal problems the couple may be having. Feelings of hostility or resentment toward her partner, for whatever reason, can make a woman unable to enjoy him in bed and must be resolved. A major goal of the treatment, in fact, is to foster communication and trust between the partners. Not only must both be willing to participate in the treatment but they must also be highly motivated to help each other out every step of the way.

The first part of the treatment—mutual stimulation without intercourse—is particularly important for women who have never experienced orgasm. It is at this point that a woman learns to recognize the sensations of sexual pleasure, in many cases for the first time. She points out to her partner exactly what stimulates her, especially in regard to specific genital manipulation, instead of just letting him do only what he thinks she enjoys. Nondemanding cooperation on the part of the man is, of course, necessary. When they attempt intercourse, the man reclines and the woman sits on top of him. In this way she controls all aspects of the penetration and regulates the action to provide herself with as much pleasure as possible. Very often the man must acquire greater control over ejaculation so that they can prolong intercourse, which will only intensify his own pleasure while giving the woman enough time to reach orgasm herself. At any time that the man feels he is about to ejaculate before they are both ready for it, the woman can remove his penis and use the squeeze technique described above. In this way the treatments for these two frequently related problems can be combined. Therapy for orgasmic dysfunction was successful in 80 percent of the cases treated by Masters and Johnson.

Masters and Johnson's overall success rate, including patients treated for a variety of sexual problems, was a remarkable

74.5 percent. These results are particularly impressive when one realizes that as recently as 1967, clinicians were reporting virtually no success at all in the treatment of premature ejaculation and "frigidity." Now these methods are being used successfully to help people overcome the same problems in homosexual relationships. Clearly, in the area of sexual dysfunction, the behavioral method is the only one that really works.

The treatments for anxiety we've described so far have all made use, in one form or another, of desensitization techniques. But there are still more anxiety-related problems that relaxation training alone, without the use of desensitization, can alleviate. The discomfort of general high tension, and the headaches that may result from it, can often be relieved by what is known as *conditioned relaxation*. The patient first learns the technique of deep muscle relaxation. When totally relaxed, he concentrates on a specific cue word, such as "calm" or "relax." The state of deep relaxation is paired with the cue word fifteen or more times during each session with the therapist over a period of four or five weeks, as well as twenty or more times every day during the client's practice sessions at home. As a result, the client becomes able to induce relaxation at once, merely by thinking of the cue word. This skill is not restricted to the therapist's office or the patient's home, but can be practiced during any stressful situation in the course of the day. If a crisis in the office arises, he can take a minute and relax; he can relax before stepping out to speak in front of an audience; he can relax during a final exam. At the first sign of a headache he can think of the cue word and relax, and prevent the headache from occurring. Many people who have had this training report a decrease in tension and anxiety in general, not only because they can reduce tension in specific situations but because they have a new sense of control over many of the difficulties of modern life.

The only danger associated with relaxation training is that it can sometimes backfire when used without the guidance of an experienced professional. An undocumented story tells of a star college basketball player who complained of excessive anxiety before and during important games. Some beginning psychology students heard about his problem, and eager to try out some of the new skills they had been learning, approached the athlete with the offer of using systematic desensitization to reduce his anxiety. He readily agreed. They taught him progressive relaxation, and then paired up the relaxation with pre-game and game-playing stimuli. As a result, he became so relaxed that he could hardly play at all, and the team went into a losing streak. Like the Sorcerer's Apprentice, the psychology students had let loose their skills before they knew how to control them. The anxiety they had eliminated was appropriate, and if they'd known better, they would have left it alone.

But such misuse is extremely rare, and the treatment of anxiety-related disorders is one area in which behavior modification is remarkably effective. Rates of 80 percent success are uncommonly high for the treatment of any problem. Of particular importance is the fact that anxiety can be relieved without the use of drugs. With the exception of the drug companies who make tranquilizers, our society as a whole can only benefit if these techniques become more widespread.

VII

The Case of Eleanor: Behavior Modification and the Neurotic

We have seen how behavior modification can be used to deal with very specific, easily pinpointed problems. But psychotherapists are also making use of behavioral techniques to help people who are just generally unhappy, or "neurotic." The story of Eleanor is a case we have fabricated to demonstrate how behavior modification works with an individual who is able to function, but is unhappy enough to seek professional help. Though the case does not involve every technique in current use, it does exemplify the basic strategy and approach that are the hallmarks of behavior therapy.

When Eleanor first appears in Dr. Mary Jones's office her attitude is cynical, almost to the point of hostility. She is a small woman in her mid-twenties, and attractive. "I've been in therapy before," she explains. "It never did any good. It just doesn't have anything to do with my problems. But my friends keep telling me I still need therapy, and maybe they're right, because everything is rotten, so I decided to try something different."

The way Dr. Jones, a behaviorally oriented psychotherapist, begins her treatment ("Tell me about yourself; why do you think you need therapy? . . . What's wrong?") is not much different from the way any other therapist would begin.

No different, Eleanor is probably thinking and she launches easily into her story, as though she had told it many times before. "Basically I'm just not very happy. In fact, I'm depressed most of the time. But why shouldn't I be? I'm an all-around flop. Men aren't attracted to me, I'm so homely and dumpy. That's why all this therapy business is so silly—you can't make me look like Ursula Andress, so what difference does it make what anyone tells me? I'm not very good at anything. I'm not especially bright and I don't get along with people that well. Men are always noticing my girl friends but not me."

Dr. Jones replies, "Okay. But I'd like you to try to be more specific. I'd like to know when you're unhappy, and what things make you feel unhappy. I'd like to know how you're living now, what your life is like, in detail."

"It's not a question of *when;* I'm always unhappy. But anyway . . ." And then Eleanor goes on to describe her life. She may claim that she is not attractive to men, but she is in fact living with one, Jeff, whom she met in college.

Besides regretting that she doesn't look like Ursula Andress, Eleanor hates her job and is bored by it, and has trouble keeping her mind on anything. She also reports that she feels physically "rotten" most of the time, but none of the doctors she's been to can find anything wrong. "Maybe it's a spastic colon," she says lightly. At any rate, she suffers from frequent abdominal pains, which no drugs seem to alleviate.

Her relationship with her boyfriend Jeff "stinks." "I mean, it's not even really a relationship. We live together and sleep together and everything, but we're basically unhappy with each other. And we fight all the time. It's always been like this with every man I've ever been with." Eleanor sighs again. Now her toughness has diminished; she seems about to cry.

"It's not only that I'm not tall, thin and pretty, and men aren't attracted to me. They just don't like me. I've never had a good relationship and I never will."

Now Dr. Jones has a general picture of Eleanor's situation and it is at this point that her methods will begin to differ from those of the therapists Eleanor has seen before. It would be very easy for Dr. Jones (as it would in fact be for all of us in this psychology-minded age) to begin making a lot of generalizations: Eleanor has an inferiority complex, is an underachiever and doesn't like herself. But Dr. Jones does not do this. She makes no effort at this point to analyze or interpret at all. And she has no intentions of unraveling Eleanor's childhood anxieties and conflicts. Her first step will be to determine what Eleanor wants out of therapy.

"Yes," Dr. Jones begins. "I can understand how painful some of what you've told me is. I believe that your problems are caused by the way you behave, the things you actually do; and right now I'm not interested in *why* you do certain things, I just want to know specifically *what* you do and *when* you do it. I'd like you to start trying to think about it in those terms during the next few weeks. To be aware of when you are the most unhappy as well as when you are *not* unhappy, and what happens right before and right after it. Do you think you can look at it that way?"

"I don't know. I suppose I can try. Why not?"

What Dr. Jones has done is to begin by trying to determine the problem. Her questions are out front, with no subtle, hidden meanings. To better understand the situation, the therapist might observe the patient in the natural, everyday environment. With a child who has trouble getting along in school, the therapist might actually go into the classroom and watch what happens. When this is not feasible, as is the case with Eleanor, the patient does the observing. Dr. Jones even asks her to count the frequency of different types of behavior in different situations, and to keep records.

The detailed examination of Eleanor's environment—her response to certain situations, as well as the consequences of her behavior—continues over the first couple of sessions. As the assessment progresses her *specific* troublesome behavior patterns become more apparent. She has tantrums, for one thing. "Jeff is always late," she says. "It makes me so *furious*. I just can't help it, he's so irresponsible, I scream at him . . . Then, I guess . . . a lot of the time I cry."

The consequences of her tantrum behavior are not simple. When she screams at Jeff he begins by vaguely defending himself, then becomes apologetic, and finally abject and comforting, especially when she cries. But she also has two very close friends, a young married couple, who respond differently. If she starts to throw a tantrum when she is with them, they often cut her off, and if she does not stop, they ask her to leave.

"I know I'm a bitch, I know I'm horrible," she confesses with a wry little smile. "But at least I admit it." Besides, being a bitch gets her reinforcement from Jeff.

It turns out that her stomach pains are directly tied to certain situations. Eleanor's observations show it in black-and-white on her notebook page labeled *Stomach:* "8 P.M. Saturday night in car with Jeff on way to party." "2 P.M. Saturday keeping Jeff company in apartment he's painting." "1 P.M. Wednesday shopping at Saks with Sarah."

Eleanor quickly recognizes the connections and says, "It seems like I get them when—it sounds so stupid and obvious —when I have to do something I don't want to do, or when somebody's making some kind of demand on me."

At the party there will no doubt be tall, thin girls who will flirt with Jeff; she is bored sitting in that empty apartment; she thinks that Sarah is prettier than she is, and that clothes look better on her. In all of these instances, the stomach aches enable her to avoid such painful situations, they give her the right to go home and lie around and do nothing, and they elicit comfort and solicitude from others. They are, in other words, being abundantly reinforced by her social environment.

Dr. Jones is also interested in finding out when good things happen. The specific aim of the initial assessment is to determine what situations in the environment are reinforcing the problem behaviors, and what situations are reinforcing any instances of the desired behaviors. Only when the antecedents and consequences are determined can the therapist know how to alter the environment in a way that will discourage the problem behavior and encourage the desired behavior.

It is often much more difficult for clients to pinpoint their positive behaviors. Not until the fourth session does Eleanor come up with anything complimentary about herself at all. "Well, sometimes Jeff and I laugh a lot. I guess I can say things he thinks are funny. My friends say that I can be witty, too, when I'm not in a bad mood."

Not only does Eleanor have a good sense of humor, she has a sense of adventure as well. Sometimes she instigates rather wild, spur-of-the-moment expeditions; what's more, she often insists on funding the entire venture. Nevertheless, Eleanor reports that her moods fluctuate abruptly. In the middle of one of her own expeditions she may believe Jeff is flirting with another girl, or decide that someone has insulted her in some way, or feel left out of the conversation. She will then begin to sulk, or develop stomach pains. If she is not taken home at once, she will then very effectively ruin the rest of the occasion for Jeff.

Though Dr. Jones makes no in-depth analysis of Eleanor's childhood, she finds out that Eleanor's behavior with men began forming at home, with the help of her father and elder brother. She was treated as the little darling of the family (they still always call her "Toodles"), and when she did not get what she wanted, the tantrums and the physical complaints would usually work. She learned so well, in fact, that even now she often self-righteously insists that her unreasonable demands are totally justified. But not all the time. In more lucid moments she will admit, with her wry little smile, that she is unreasonably selfish. And it is during one of these moments that Dr. Jones suggests to Eleanor that she bring Jeff to their next session. "He's a very important person in your life—he has a great effect on how you behave. Unless we get Jeff into the picture, we'll have a hard time getting things changed."

Enter Jeff. For the first time Eleanor is late for her appointment. Jeff is a good-looking, rather shambling young man with nervous fingers; he is uncomfortable and monosyllabic. Dr. Jones explains what she is trying to do in her assessment of Eleanor's situation and Jeff's part in it. She also asks Jeff about himself. It turns out that Jeff's past girl friends were docile and undemanding, not like Eleanor at all, and none of them lasted for more than a few months. In fact, his mother, who is very critical and domineering, is the only other woman he's ever had to deal with for an extended period of time. He says he really loves Eleanor and wants to make her happy but he just doesn't know how.

"What seems to make Eleanor upset?" Dr. Jones asks.

"Well, I'm not really sure," Jeff says, pondering the question. "I know sometimes it's me. I have a hard time getting organized—that usually means that I'm slow about getting things done and that makes her mad. I have really tried, but somehow I'm always holding things up."

"You make it sound like I never do anything wrong," Eleanor says, almost humorously. "You know I'm a bitch. Admit it! Anybody who could put up with me has to be a real creep."

At first glance it appears that this case has *disproved* the Law of Effect. After all, here are two people who are stubbornly remaining in an unpleasant situation and continuing to behave in ways that make them both unhappy. The behaviorists claim that the Law of Effect applies to all of our behavior, that it applies even to the most extreme psychotic behavior. Are Eleanor and Jeff, with their not so unfamiliar problems, enough to knock down the behaviorists' house of cards?

No. Convincing behavioral hypotheses can be offered to explain Eleanor's behavior. Being a bitch—giving out punishment—worked with her father and brother; it works with Jeff and it even works with most of her friends, who let her get away with it simply because she makes things unpleasant for them if they don't. It's behavior that is reinforced, and it continues. She also gives out reinforcement (being charming, being fun to be with), which is why it is possible for her to maintain her familiar, bitchy behavior without being ostracized by everybody.

Then there are those friends who do not tolerate her tantrums. By actual count Eleanor herself has discovered that since therapy began she has far fewer tantrums when she is with them than when she is with others. In behavioral terms, they are stimuli that signal no reinforcement for bitchiness. If she doesn't want to drive them away, she must either compromise or get her own way by more positive methods, such as charm and persuasion. Since this relationship continues (indeed, she considers these people her best friends), it seems that these particular skills are, to some small extent, already a part of her behavioral repertoire.

And now on to Jeff. Another therapist could very easily label him as "masochistic": he continues to live with a woman who browbeats and criticizes him, and complicates his life by expecting him to carry out unreasonable demands and favors, and if she does not actually prevent him from attending parties or social events which he would enjoy, she will either capriciously drag him away from them or else cast such a pall of black gloom over the entire occasion that everyone is made to suffer. But Dr. Jones doesn't use such labels. As a behaviorist she most likely feels that diagnostic labels don't help her understand what's going on or how to correct things. They may identify certain patterns of behavior, but that is all they do— a label is not a solution.

Instead, she tries to determine what is reinforcing Jeff's behavior. To begin with, from the information Dr. Jones has about Jeff she can zero right in on the fact that he has had a lot of practice dealing with a critical, domineering woman: his mother. It's the kind of relationship in which he may well feel the most comfortable, and not only by virtue of its familiarity and the years he has spent learning how to handle it. Such a situation can also provide certain not so obvious, but nevertheless extremely reinforcing, benefits. For one thing, he's always the good guy. No matter what havoc this poor unhappy girl

may wreak upon him, he responds almost always with tender-
ness and comfort. She's unfair and takes advantage of him; he
tries to make her feel good and help her out. In the eyes of
himself and the world he turns the other cheek, ignores his own
suffering and does whatever he can to bring some happiness
into her life. A role that gets heavily reinforced, right? He's a
martyr, a nice guy and a kind person.

Or at least that is how he appears. But according to a
behavioral analysis, he is really not a nice guy at all. His martyr-
like behavior actually reinforces her tantrums and is instrumen-
tal in maintaining her bitchiness. But even if Jeff realized that,
he might continue to give in because the immediate positive
consequences of appeasing her (i.e., she stops screaming) are
more powerful than the long-range aversive ones (i.e., she continues using tantrums to get her own way).

Jeff also gets companionship and security out of the relationship; he gets someone to come home to; he gets someone
who is occasionally fun to be with. Plus, he gets the comfort
of a familiar situation that we've already discussed. So he's not
really a "masochist" at all. On his own personal scale, the
reinforcement he gets from the relationship outweighs the
punishment. And so he stays.

Dr. Jones and Eleanor now have a complete enough understanding of Eleanor's environment for them to start establishing a mutually agreeable set of goals for the treatment. She
has explained to Eleanor that she does not approach the case
with an already established picture of what her client "should"
be like when therapy is over. All she wants is to help Eleanor
solve what she herself considers her problems, and that does
not always mean trying to make her conform to society's view
of what a "normal" person should be like. If someone sent a
truly "happy hooker" to Dr. Jones, for example, she would not
necessarily try to get her to change professions. (A happy ax
murderess, however, or anyone else who was a threat to society,
would be a different story.)

Eleanor and Dr. Jones have no trouble at all agreeing on

the goal of getting rid of Eleanor's stomach pains. Nor does it take them much time to agree that Eleanor would like to be less depressed and learn how to be a bit more diplomatic and *not* have tantrums every time things don't go just the way she wants.

"I really believe that you can learn how to get along better with people," Dr. Jones says. "And since Jeff is willing to help, we can start with that relationship. Moreover, learning how to get along with Jeff will help you in your relationships with other people, men as well as women."

But just "to get along with Jeff" is still not specific enough. Dr. Jones explains that they must pick out specific types of behavior in specific situations to work on. Here is a brief list of a few of the problems that Eleanor presents, and the behavioral goals they set up.

SITUATION: Jeff is late picking her up.
   Problem Behavior: Eleanor throws a screaming fit and Jeff tries to make up.
   Behavioral Goal: A pleasant ride home without a fight.

SITUATION: They are at a party and Jeff is talking and laughing with a tall, pretty girl.
   Problem Behavior: Eleanor pulls Jeff into another room, sulks, insists that her stomach hurts and that they leave the party.
   Behavioral Goal: Eleanor either ignores what Jeff is doing and continues her own conversation or else joins Jeff and the girl and talks pleasantly with them.

SITUATION: Eleanor is at a friend's house and she wants to leave.
   Problem Behavior: Eleanor phones Jeff and demands that he come and pick her up at once, no matter what he is doing.
   Behavioral Goal: Eleanor gets home on her own, without disturbing Jeff.

In this step of the treatment, Dr. Jones asks Eleanor to *be aware* of the situations that elicit her bad behavior, and to try to think of alternate and more constructive ways to behave in these situations. Certainly, doing this will help her to obtain a little objectivity about her own actions and will enable her to exert a bit of control over how she responds.

But just thinking of new ways to behave isn't enough. The list of goals lacks the most vital element for change: the consequences. In order for her behavior to change, Eleanor must get *more* reinforcement for her new behavior pattern than she did for the old. Of course, in many situations by just being pleasant instead of a bitch, she will naturally be more likely to get pleasantness in return, which is reinforcing to a certain degree. But with Jeff this is not necessarily the case. The two of them are firmly rooted in a pattern of reinforcing each other's maladaptive behavior. If she is going to change, Jeff must learn to reinforce her new behavior patterns and not reinforce her old and destructive ones. In other words, he has to change as well. There is no avoiding the fact that it is a two-way street, and this is what makes it so hard. Everyone involved has to modify his or her own behavior in order to correct the problem.

Dr. Jones goes on to explain this to Eleanor and Jeff and to point out that it isn't easy to change one's ways of behaving. "Of course, it's difficult to put changes like that into effect," she tells them. "I'm certainly not going to promise that we can solve all your problems. This kind of therapy has its limitations, just like any other. There's no such thing as a miracle cure. But even though we can't make it exactly effortless, there are some methods you can use that do make it easier to change your environment and your responses to it. There are certain things you can do that really help when problem situations crop up. One of them is to devise what we call *contingency contracts*— and that involves both of you. We may have to try some other things as well, but I'd like to help you set up some contracts together during the next few sessions."

Dr. Jones explains that a behavioral contingency contract

is exactly what it sounds like: an agreement (if necessary, written down and signed by both) that in a specific "situation" one party promises to behave in a particular way and in return the other party promises to respond to that behavior in a particular way. Included are both positive and negative types of behavior and responses.

To help understand how contracting works, we can look at the especially clear example of how it can be used to improve family relations. For example, the parents of a boy who's flunking out of seventh grade might agree to let him and his friends have exclusive access to the color TV and game room on Saturday evening if he'll show them his completed homework every night. Or they might make a bargain with their fifteen-year-old daughter who weighs 79 pounds and exists on a diet of water and low-calorie imitation cottage cheese: they will quit making nasty comments about her clothes and excuse her from her usual kitchen chores if she'll eat at least one regular meal a day. Even young children can understand the idea of a simple contract and will fulfill the terms of it surprisingly well. Not only does this kind of bargaining help eliminate particular problems, it also establishes clear lines of communication.

But of course, contracts are easier to make than they are to keep. So Eleanor and Jeff decide to have their first contract deal with the very clear-cut problem of Eleanor's stomach aches, or at least her complaining about them. Since the initial assessment seems to indicate that the stomach pains are related to the situation she is in, Dr. Jones feels optimistic about the chances of success with a behavioral treatment program. But before she embarks on such a program, she checks with Eleanor's regular physician and verifies that there are no medical bases for her problem. As far as the doctor is concerned, Dr. Jones should proceed with her plans. So Dr. Jones helps Eleanor and Jeff set up a contingency contract. For each week that Eleanor does not complain about her stomach pains, Jeff agrees to spend the following Saturday with her in any way she wants. If Eleanor wants to stay home and play Scrabble instead of going to a party, Jeff will happily agree. They will spend the whole day in bed, if that is what she wants. If she does complain about her stomach, he will remind her of the contract and give her another chance. But if she complains again, she forfeits the Saturday privileges, plus she has to do all the food shopping and laundry for the week. It is really quite a simple agreement.

After three weeks Eleanor and Jeff come into the office in a noticeably brighter mood. "I guess it must have been the contract," Eleanor says. "I mean, it was hard at first not to talk about the pain, but now, it seems like I just don't even notice it that much. I still get them, but not as often. Jeff only had to remind me about the contract twice."

More confident now, they want to tackle the more complex problem of their relationship. But before they begin to discuss another contract, Dr. Jones emphasizes that they must remember to maintain this one if the stomach pains are to continue to diminish. As before, Dr. Jones suggests that they focus on something specific—like Eleanor's tantrums.

The new contract provides ways that Jeff can reinforce Eleanor for expressing herself more constructively and not have tantrums. If she does when they are at home, Jeff is to walk out; if they are driving in the car, Jeff is to pull off the road and wait for her to stop. In no case is Jeff to try to appease her or give in to her demands. And every day that she does not have a tantrum, he agrees to give her a ride to work the next day. Furthermore, the same rules about Saturdays apply to her tantrums as her stomach complaints. If she does not throw a tantrum, the day is hers; if she does, she's got all the laundry and shopping to do. It may seem that Jeff is doing most of the work, but if the contract is successful, he will be reaping the obvious benefit of not being yelled at all the time.

They are not so enthusiastic when they arrive at the office a week later. "It didn't work," Eleanor explains succinctly as she deposits the torn shreds of the contract on Dr. Jones's desk.

"Well, tell me what happened," Dr. Jones says, "and maybe we can figure out how to make a better contract."

"I tried for a couple of days, I really did," Eleanor says.

"And Jeff did drive me to work. But then on Wednesday night he was late picking me up again." She glares at Jeff, who shrugs and looks away from her. "I mean, I just couldn't control myself. Anyway, I *deserved* to be mad at him, didn't I?"

"I don't know," Dr. Jones says. "But we did include the possibility of your getting angry in the contract. What happened after that?"

"The usual," Eleanor says. "I screamed at him and he kept apologizing. I mean, why should I let him stop the car? It was his fault. He was late."

Dr. Jones turns to Jeff. "I know how difficult it is to try to change long-standing patterns, like the way you respond to anger. It takes a while, and you shouldn't be discouraged. But it might help if you could tell me what was going on in your mind when it happened. Did you remember the contract at all, did you try to behave differently?"

"Yes, I remembered it," Jeff says uncomfortably. "But I really couldn't help being late. I had to stay at work until I finished this job that turned out to be trickier than I thought it would. And I tried to call Eleanor but I couldn't reach her. So when I finally got there I kept trying to explain and saying 'Remember the contract, I'm going to have to pull over,' and she said—"

"I said, 'Screw the contract!' " Eleanor interrupts.

"I mean, I just couldn't do it," Jeff says. "I thought if I pulled over she'd just keep on screaming." He lifts his hands hopelessly.

Though Eleanor is clearly being unfair, she is, in one sense, correct about the failure of the contract. As Dr. Jones pointed out, it was assumed that she might have tantrums. What went wrong was Jeff's response. Once again, he reinforced her maladaptive behavior. As long as he goes on doing that, she'll go on having tantrums. Only if Jeff stops giving in so that Eleanor does not get reinforcement for the behavior is there any hope that her behavior will change. But there is nothing in the contract that makes it any easier than before for Jeff not to give in.

The contract also leaves Eleanor in the lurch. While it specifies that she is not to be reinforced for having tantrums, it doesn't give her any positive behavior to use instead. It makes it no easier for Jeff to resist, and no easier for Eleanor to refrain. Indeed, if such contracts were Dr. Jones's only therapeutic tool, she would not be able to help them much at all. But she has other tools, which, to be effective, she uses along with the contracts. She reasons that it would be to their advantage to learn certain valuable behavioral skills which they lack—specifically, how to assert their own needs constructively and effectively when they conflict with the needs of others. In most situations Eleanor only knows how to scream; Jeff only knows how to give in.

Eleanor, we have already seen, does have some alternatives to her tantrums, but only when she is with her friends the married couple. And as it turns out, Jeff does know how to assert himself when it's easy. But the moment there is a threat of anger, or even the suggestion of displeasure, he will back down. Hence, it is not unusual for people to take advantage of him.

The technique Dr. Jones uses to help each of them strengthen his very limited skill in dealing with conflict is assertiveness training, and we can take a more detailed look at how this training works in Jeff's case. She begins by explaining to him the whole procedure and the rationale behind it. As we have described, it consists essentially of giving Jeff the opportunity to get practice in her office at being assertive. They will use role playing; sometimes Jeff will act as himself and Dr. Jones will take the part of the person he is in conflict with. They will also do it the other way around, so that Dr. Jones can give examples of assertive behavior and Jeff can get a feeling of the effect his own assertive behavior might have on another person. This step is important because nonassertive people often have unrealistic expectations of the effects their own assertive behavior might have. By putting themselves in the other person's position they can realize how unrealistic their expectations are.

But just playacting in the therapist's office is not the whole solution, so Dr. Jones will instruct Jeff in how to put his skills into practice in real life. He will first try out his assertive behavior in situations in which there is very little chance that he will not succeed. When he is comfortable being assertive in this type of situation, Dr. Jones will teach him how to express his needs in situations where he might encounter resistance. As he progresses through the training Dr. Jones will keep close track of his performance in real-life situations. If he continues to succeed at being assertive, she can move him on more rapidly, but if he experiences any failure, she will stop and analyze what went wrong and then give Jeff the needed training to prevent the problem from recurring. Training is a gradual process; optimally his assertive behavior will be reinforced at every stage. Once again it's the Law of Effect. If the program is arranged so that being assertive is a way for him to get reinforcement and to avoid punishment, then Jeff will become more assertive.

This gradual step-by-step approach to therapy and skill training is one of the hallmarks of behavior modification. Regardless of the problem or the client, the therapist always begins with a very easy task. Only after the client has mastered one step does he progress to the next. And to make sure that the therapy program is appropriate, the therapist carefully monitors the client's progress. If the client experiences any difficulty, the therapist revises his program so that he can learn the necessary skills. The aim is for the client to experience success at every stage.

After several weeks of assertiveness training, Jeff reports an incident to Dr. Jones. "I was just getting out of work and it was five o'clock and raining. I was supposed to meet Eleanor. Anyway, we have this secretary . . . Eleanor hates her, of course, because she's really thin and looks like a model. When I left work she was standing at the door without an umbrella. She smiled and asked if I could help her."

"And what did you do?" Dr. Jones asks.

"Well, I knew I had to leave right away to meet Eleanor.

I guess I should have been assertive and just told Kathy that I was sorry but I had to get somewhere right away. But I was afraid she might hold it against me, and anyway, I like her and didn't want to just leave her stranded there in the pouring rain. So I helped her get a cab. It took forever and so I was late picking up Eleanor. But I didn't know what else to do. Does being assertive mean you have to be lousy to other people, like leaving Kathy stranded there?"

"No, it doesn't. But it does mean balancing your own needs with theirs, and trying to come up with solutions that don't always make things worse for you. Did you try to explain your situation to Kathy at all?"

"No . . . I mean, it just would have sounded lousy of me."

"Well, put yourself in her place for a moment. How do you think she would have felt if you had said something like 'I'd really like to help you get a cab, Kathy, but I've got to be downtown right away and I'm already late. You can borrow my umbrella if you want; I don't really need it. Or maybe you could call a cab and just wait for it here?' "

"You know, I never thought of that at all," Jeff says.

"Do you think Kathy would have been angry if you'd said that to her?"

"I don't see how she could be."

"When you're faced with a situation like that, it often helps to think of some alternative that doesn't involve your putting yourself out unfairly to someone else's advantage. If you can come up with another suggestion, they won't be as likely to keep putting the pressure on you. And it always helps to explain your own situation, too."

As therapy progresses, Jeff gradually learns how to be more assertive in general, and with Eleanor in particular. And the fact that Eleanor is also receiving assertiveness training makes the process of change smoother for them both. With role playing and practice in real-life situations, she gradually begins to learn some alternatives to the tantrums, which were just as unpleasant for her as they were for everyone else. It's a process that is naturally reinforcing, for the attention and affection that she craves from others only become more and more accessible as she learns to be more diplomatic, and even to be aware, occasionally, of the other person's point of view. But this is not the only benefit Eleanor receives. Being assertive for her also means being more comfortable in previously distressing situations, such as those in which she feels she is being unfavorably compared to other women. Her good humor and acerbic wit, which she has usually only been able to exhibit when she is with Jeff and her very close friends, can be generalized through the training, so that she can make use of it at parties, for example. By getting people to laugh and enjoy themselves, she can get just as much attention—even from men—as the girls who (she thinks) are more attractive than she is.

With both of them receiving assertiveness training, the contract becomes a decidedly more feasible proposition, since both of them are learning the skills required to fulfill it. After several months of the training, in fact, the contract is still intact—though just barely.

"In one way I really wanted to go to that party," Eleanor explains to Dr. Jones. But I knew there were going to be all these gorgeous girls. Also"—she looks over at Jeff—"I did scream at Jeff during the week. Not as bad as before but . . . He had the right to go to the party without me, according to the contract. Anyway, I decided I really wanted to go, so we went. Maybe he shouldn't have taken me, but—"

"It just seemed stupid not to take her," Jeff puts in. "I mean, the fight was minor, it wasn't like before. And I *wanted* her to come, so I was still doing what *I* wanted. It really didn't seem like I was breaking the contract. Do you think it was a mistake?"

"Not necessarily," Dr. Jones says. "It depends on what happened. So what happened?"

"Well," Eleanor goes on, "We got there and it really was fun at first. Just running around the house and seeing all these different types. But then I started feeling out of it, and there were all these girls that looked like models and it was like nobody cared that I was there, and for a while I couldn't even find Jeff. So then I wanted to leave and my stomach started to hurt, so I went and found him and he was talking to these people I didn't know. And I said I didn't feel good and I wanted to go."

"And I told her I thought she was making a mistake," Jeff says assertively. "I said she would probably like the people I was talking to, but if she insisted on leaving, she could go. I was having a good time and I was staying."

Eleanor picks up the story again. "So I started getting really mad and frustrated, and I went and got my coat, and got his coat, and I was going to go where he was and thrust his coat at him and *make* him take me home. I kept thinking, I'm not supposed to do this, but I also kept thinking, big deal, he *has* to take me home."

"Suddenly there was Eleanor," Jeff goes on, "standing next to me with my coat and her coat. At first I was afraid she might make a scene, but then I realized that she probably wouldn't do it in front of a whole room of strangers. Usually she takes me into the bedroom or bathroom and then gets upset. So I figured if I didn't move, it wouldn't happen. I took our coats and put them in the corner, and then introduced her to the people I was talking to."

"Then one of them, this guy, asked me what I was doing with the coats," Eleanor continues. "So I told him I thought we were going to leave but we couldn't because we had this stupid contract. So they all wanted to know about the contract, and I started telling them . . . but not really. I made it sound crazy and funny and I didn't tell any of the embarrassing parts."

"They were really laughing," Jeff adds. "They'd never heard anything like it before. And then somebody asked her if she wanted another drink, and in the end I wanted to leave before she did."

"Of course, I got mad at him on the way home," Eleanor goes on rather defensively. "I mean, even though I had a good time, I was still mad at him. My stomach really *did* hurt, he acted like it was nothing, like I was just making it up. And then he stopped the car and that made me even madder. But then—"

"But what could I do?" Jeff asks and shrugs apologetically. "It was two A.M. We couldn't just sit there. I just shut up and drove her home while she screamed." He pauses. "But one thing is for sure," he says, turning to Eleanor. "Next Saturday is *mine*. And you've got a lot of dirty clothes to wash."

"But that's not fair!" Eleanor cries. A moment later, Dr. Jones steps in. Therapy continues.

Behavior modification is characterized by a careful analysis of the factors in the patient's social environment that evoke, reinforce and punish adaptive as well as maladaptive behavior. The aim of therapy is to change those factors to modify his behavior. And the goals, we emphasize once more, are those of the patient.

VIII

Behavior Modification and the Psychotic

Over 600,000 people in the United States suffer from severe psychological disorders. These people include children as young as eighteen months who withdraw and become rigid when held, appearing to reject all love and affection, as well as adults who are withdrawn and depressed, unable to separate fact from fantasy. With diagnoses such as autism, organic brain syndrome and schizophrenia, at least half of these people reside in large state-run mental institutions. Treatment can take years. In fact, the majority of the patients in psychiatric hospitals at the present time have lived there for more than five years, and it is not at all unusual to find people on back wards who have been hospitalized for forty or fifty years. The prognoses for most of these people are dismal.

The cost in personal suffering defies estimation. There are some families in which two or more individuals have been institutionalized for years. The price of treatment itself is staggering. Individual psychotherapy usually costs at least $50 an hour, and hospitalization can easily exceed $20,000 a year. In an article appearing in the September 1975 issue of the *American Journal of Psychiatry*, Drs. John Dunderson and Loren Mosher reported that schizophrenia alone annually costs our society between $11.6 billion $19.6 billion. They also pointed out in their report that there is absolutely no reason to expect these figures to decrease in the near future. In fact, most authorities believe that they will increase.

Great effort has been directed toward understanding these disorders. As early as the late 1800's, whole textbooks focused on abnormal psychology. But unfortunately, we have made little progress. There is not even a clear consensus among authorities as to what characterizes psychotic disorders. With disturbed children there is often an almost total rejection of other people—it is sometimes even difficult to get them to look directly at you. Psychotic adults often have vivid hallucinations —they report hearing music and voices and often claim that they communicate with deceased relatives or people from outer space.

In order to give some idea of the complexity and bizarreness of these disorders, we will present two cases. One is a child; the other an adult. The first case is taken from the book, *A Child Called Noah,* Josh Greenfeld's account of his struggle to help his son. The passage we have selected describes an incident in a supermarket involving Noah, his father and a friendly woman who stops to greet the cute little boy.

> "What's your name?" she asks the boy. He turns his head away, making some unintelligible sounds. "What's your name?" she asks again. The boy begins to rock back and forth in the shopping cart. "Don't be shy," the woman continues. "Can't you tell me your name?"
>
> "No," says the father, "he can't."
>
> The woman looks up with sudden concern. "Doesn't he talk?"
>
> "Not anymore," says the father.

"I'm sorry," says the woman, gently reaching out to pat the boy, who ducks his head away.

"What's the matter with him? He's so beautiful."

"We don't know," replies the father.

"Oh"—the woman recovers her natural jovialty—"don't worry. Whatever is bothering him, he'll grow out of it, I'm sure."

I wish I could be sure. The boy is my son Noah.

At the age of four Noah is neither toilet-trained nor does he feed himself. He seldom speaks expressively, rarely employs his less-than-a-dozen-word vocabulary. His attention span in a new toy is a matter of split seconds, television engages him for only an odd moment occasionally, he is never interested in other children for very long. His main activities are lint-catching, thread-pulling, blanket-sucking, spontaneous giggling, inexplicable crying, eye-squinting, wall-hugging, circle-walking, bed-bouncing, jumping, rocking, door closing, and incoherent babbling addressed to his finger-flexing right hand.[1]

The second case is taken from *Patterns of Psychopathology*, by Drs. Melvin Zax and George Stricker. The patient is a twenty-four-year-old man admitted to a large mental hospital.

He entered the municipal hospital with a self-inflicted mutilation of his penis, done in order that he could get his girl friend pregnant at a distance. While being treated for this wound he discussed, at great length, the special symbolism of words and numbers, interrupting himself to laugh inappropriately at times. He also volunteered the information that he was sick because dwarfs had stuck him with green needles. . . . An example of an interview with Robert follows.

Doctor: What are you talking about?

Robert: I've been lured, I've been lured time and time again. I've been lured by mobs and lured by money to build space. They talk about pleasure principle, pleasure purpose, it's merely false sex.

Doctor: What do you mean?

Robert: I know what I'm doing. I'm living out my grandfather's life. They had to tell me, my mother went. America sees its own heirs.

Doctor: Does God talk to you?

Robert: No, I don't get voices. I just used that for a sex point.

Doctor: Do you see some particular pattern for the world?

Robert: It's immaterial. I don't say I can't use the moon. God made the moon so let it have it. I'm like a psychiatrist and I'm trying to help my mother.

Doctor: What's wrong with her?

Robert: I've got intuition. She doesn't seem to want to be a father. If she'd show me a written statement I'll be the priest.

Doctor: Have you ever seen any visions?

Robert: I don't see visions. I see God in word and deed. My mother couldn't stand any such program.

Doctor: What does that chair look like to you?

Robert: Sex. It's immaterial. The legs are like the moon, sexy to a point. They tell me that the clothes were divided. I want to see who's lying. They've got the greater part of the money. They live out lies. When I meet God I can live out a clean conscience.

Doctor: What do you think about sex?

Robert: It doesn't have any bearing. It's just that I'm trying to mislead people. I'm trying to get my mother straightened out.

Doctor: Has anyone bothered you?

Robert: No, I don't get visions. I don't try to keep information in my mind. That's how I know what the stars say. That's how I feel people.

Doctor: What do the stars say?

Robert: The moon's knowledge is to concentrate on a little work. God wants to see if I'm sincere.[2]

Not all severely disturbed individuals display such extreme symptoms. Some people seem to drift in and out of their confused condition, and others will sit motionless for hours, seemingly unaware of everything around them.

As one might expect, for years people have tried to explain what causes these severe disorders. In 1896 the German psychiatrist Emil Kraepelin hypothesized that a malfunction of the sex glands, producing a chemical imbalance, caused these disorders, and that this imbalance resulted in deterioration of the nervous system. Kraepelin used the term dementia praecox to refer to such disorders. He believed that the disorders originate during adolescence (hence *praecox*, meaning premature) and involve progressive mental deterioration (hence *dementia*). The term dementia praecox was later replaced by the term schizophrenia, which refers to a group of disorders involving marked disturbances in behavior, thought and emotion. It does not, as is sometimes thought, refer to a person's having two or more distinct personalities. The most striking feature is a distortion in perception of reality.

Since Kraepelin's early formulations, researchers have generated many theories regarding the causes of schizophrenia. While some behaviorists have offered their own explanations, most have avoided such speculation. They feel that medical science does not know enough about these disorders to develop theories as to what causes them. Unfortunately, they are right. To date, not only have none of the theories of mental illness been validated, none have led to a truly effective method of treatment. As we suggested earlier, the prognosis for anyone suffering from schizophrenia or some other psychotic disorder is poor.

Clearly, children like Noah provide some of the most challenging problems for all of psychiatry. Parents of these children often become painfully aware of the challenge to themselves very early in the child's life. They first think that their infant is deaf because he doesn't respond like other children. In fact, he may even appear to be ignoring them or shrinking from them. When they lean over his crib to play with or talk to him, he acts as if no one is there. For many parents it is this problem that makes them seek professional help for their child. But when they have him examined they learn that the child is not blind or deaf. At this point they are relieved, but confused as to what's wrong. With time the problem becomes more obvious. They notice that the child doesn't like to be cuddled and becomes rigid when they pick him up. He doesn't cling like a normal infant. And when he gets older he seems uninterested in affection. He doesn't cry or laugh as one would expect. He seems aloof and indifferent to people, yet may become fascinated by a tiny piece of paper fifteen feet across the room. When some object does arouse his interest, he may sit and manipulate it repetitively for hours. This behavior also carries over into stereotyped movements: the child may twirl his hair, flip his hands or rock his body over and over. His speech may also be confused and difficult to understand. Many of these children do not really communicate when they speak; they merely echo what others say. To the question "Do you want a cookie?" they might respond, "Do you want a cookie?" And most horrifying of all, many of these children inflict serious injuries on themselves. Such a child might bite himself, bang his head on sharp objects or scratch his own body until it bleeds. Children like this have even been known to blind themselves. Left to their own devises, they might literally kill themselves. Because this behavior is so unpredictable, such children may have to be heavily sedated with drugs or put into strait jackets.

Because of the incredible complexity of these disorders, psychiatrists and psychologists have great difficulty agreeing on a diagnosis for a particular child. It is not at all unusual for a child to have three or four conflicting diagnoses from different professionals. Noah, for example, had four. They ranged from brain damage to childhood schizophrenia to autism.

As one can easily understand, such a child can devastate an entire family. Not only are the parents heartbroken and distraught, but nothing they do seems to help. They have almost no freedom if he lives at home. They cannot leave him alone and usually find it impossible to hire a baby-sitter. In these cases the word "challenge" is an understatement.

Of course, there is a wealth of theories regarding the causes of the disorder. Some authorities contend that it is a perceptual problem: the child's bizarre behavior is related to his inability to receive certain types of sensory stimulation. Others claim that he suffers from specific neurological deficits that make it impossible to arouse adequately those areas of the brain responsible for processing information. And Freudians believe that the child is reacting to rejection by cold and detached parents. But no one really knows. Not only have none of these theories led to an effective method of treatment, but they have also resulted in much needless suffering. Parents have been made to feel that their behavior with the child is the cause of his disorder, when in fact there is no evidence at all for this accusation.

Behavior modifiers have tackled these problems of psychotic children in a very different manner. Certainly it would be of value to understand what causes the disorder, so that we could perhaps prevent it. But since no one does know at this point, many psychotherapists have directed their efforts toward figuring out ways to simply get rid of the bizarre behavior and encourage more appropriate ways of behaving.

One of the first and most successful cases treated with behavior modification involved a three-and-a-half-year-old boy named Dicky who was diagnosed as schizophrenic. His parents described him as perfectly normal until he developed cataracts at the age of nine months. At that time he began having violent tantrums and by three years of age his problems had become so severe that he had to be hospitalized at the Western State Hospital in Washington. Dicky's tantrums included not only crying and screaming; his head-banging, face-slapping, hair-pulling and face-scratching often left him bloody. Even sedative drugs and physical restraints did not stop his tantrums. And Dicky had other problems as well. He refused to wear the glasses that were prescribed to prevent a partial loss of vision. As soon as they were placed on his face, he would rip them off. Also a terror at meals and bedtime, he threw food, and refused to stay in bed.

The psychologists first developed a program to eliminate Dicky's tantrums. They used timeout plus positive reinforcement for good, or non-tantrum, behavior. As soon as Dicky started a tantrum they removed all sources of rewards by isolating him in an empty room. When he stopped, he was allowed to come out and return to whatever he was doing. Regardless of where he was, tantrums would result in immediate timeout. This procedure proved to be very effective; within two and a half months Dicky's tantrums were almost completely eliminated.

To get Dicky to wear his prescription glasses, the psychologists devised an elaborate shaping program. They began by rewarding him with small bits of candy and fruit for just holding a pair of glasses. By gradually being required to come closer to actually wearing the glasses, Dicky learned to accept having them on.

The staff at the hospital continued working with Dicky intensively, teaching him communication and self-help skills. At the age of four and a half he was discharged from the hospital and returned home. With the guidance of the psychologists, his parents continued the training. Then, when he was five, he was enrolled in a special behavioral preschool of the University of Washington. At the preschool he received one-to-one training in order to develop both academic and social skills. Following two years at the preschool he moved on to a public-school class for the mentally retarded, then to a class for the physically handicapped. Finally, at age ten, he was able to handle a regular classroom. In 1972, when Dicky was thirteen years old, a report was made of his progress over the ten years since the behavioral treatment program began. He now attends a public junior high school and lives at home with his family. While the psychologists point out that he still shows certain unusual types of behavior such as occasionally rocking in his seat and clapping his hands inappropriately, he has improved remarkably. He can keep up with his classmates, has a good mastery of language and is friendly and outgoing.

Other severely disturbed children often have bizarre

speech. Many of these children produce strange grunts and squeals, and some of them repeat words or phrases which may be recognizable but do not seem to apply to the situation. Because of the importance of language in development, many treatment programs begin with communication training. Usually the teacher must first get the child to pay attention. To do this the teacher begins by showing the child a piece of candy. Once he shows interest, the teacher holds it next to her eyes and says, "Look at me." As soon as the child's gaze wanders to the food, the teacher gives him the candy. After many repetitions, the child starts looking at the teacher when she speaks. The teacher then extends the length of time he must look at her each time before she gives him the food. Sometimes she may say, "Look at me," without holding the candy near her face—when the child looks at her he gets a hug and a piece of candy.

Once the child is able to concentrate on what the teacher says and does, she moves on to actually teaching the child how to speak. First she teaches him how to make basic letter sounds such as "a" and "mm." Then he must be taught to say words and put them together into sentences. He must learn to express what he wants, identify objects and follow instructions. This all takes time. Depending upon the child's ability and the teacher's skill, language training can take weeks or months of extensive one-to-one tutoring.

Parents of psychotic children have sometimes learned to work with their own child in this way. They have often proven to be the most effective therapists their children could ever have. They are with the children more than anyone else is, and can, in a sense, give them continuous treatment. Moreover, the praise and attention of the parents is more important to the children than any other therapist's could be, and therefore is one of the most powerful rewards that can be devised.

Though inability to use language is a serious handicap, the self-injury that some of these children engage in is much worse. In addition to blinding themselves by banging their faces against sharp objects, these children have actually been known to bite off parts of their fingers and to remove pieces of their own flesh with their teeth. To prevent this self-injury, many of them are literally tied down by all fours or drugged until they are zombies. In mental institutions it is not at all unusual to see a child wearing a football helmet—it is to protect his head when he bangs it against the floor. But sometimes these children figure out other ways to hurt themselves, and the restraints become worthless. In one case a disturbed child figured out how he could bang his head on the frame of the bed even though he was restrained by a special sheet—the bed had to be padded. But even if the restraints do work, they solve nothing. A child in a strait jacket hardly has much of a life.

Today the foremost authority on the treatment of autistic children and their self-destructive behavior is O. Ivar Lovaas, professor of psychology at the University of California in Los Angeles. Like many other psychotherapists working in this area, Lovaas does not have a lot of preconceived ideas about these children. He approaches each child on an individual basis and tries to come up with an effective method of changing that child's maladaptive behavior. In a recent article Lovaas noted that his approach to treating children resembles those proposed by certain practitioners more than forty years ago:

> . . . many of the procedures we have described are not new, but bear striking similarities to those described by Itard ("The Wild Boy of Aveyron") and by Sullivan [Helen Keller's teacher] (in Gibson's "The Miracle Worker") and recently by Clark ("The Siege"). We are especially struck by the similarity in their willingness to use functional consequences for the child's behaviors, the meticulous building of new behaviors in a piece-by-piece fashion, the intrustion [sic] of the education into all aspects of the child's life, the comprehensive, hour-by-hour, day-by-day commitment to the child by an adult, etc.
>
> So the principles we employ are not new. Reinforcement, like gravity, is everywhere, and has been for a long time.[3]

One of his first cases was a ten-year-old girl named Beth, diagnosed as autistic at the age of one. Like other autistic children, she was very withdrawn. She did not speak but merely parroted what was said to her. Since the age of three she had been self-destructive, biting and tearing her skin and banging her head on sharp corners of tables and chairs. After carefully observing her and recording the frequency of the self-injurious behavior, Lovaas and his colleagues consulted other professionals to find out how they would treat the problem. At that time the prevailing theory in psychiatry was that self-destructive behavior was a symptom of an underlying problem such as guilt or poor self-concept; the child abuses herself because she feels guilty or worthless. The psychiatrists suggested that the therapist lavish love on her in order to help her change her self-concept and thereby eliminate the problem behavior. And the most important time to do this was when she felt the worst about herself; that is, when she was abusing herself. The psychiatrists suggested that as soon as Beth started hitting herself, the therapist give her reassurance by telling her how much he cared for her. In order to determine if their recommendations were valid, Lovaas tried it. If they were correct, then she should stop hitting herself; if they were wrong, her behavior should either get worse or go unchanged. Since he had a detailed record of her prior self-destructive behavior and could continue to record her behavior during treatment, it was easy for him to evaluate the effectiveness of the psychiatrists' recommendations.

All Lovaas had to do was compare the number of times she hit herself before, after and during treatment. When he made these simple comparisons, the results were startlingly clear. On those days that the therapists reassured her whenever she hurt herself, she became worse—the frequency of self-injurious behavior increased dramatically. When they stopped giving reassurance she got better—the frequency returned to the pretreatment level. Lovaas tested the psychiatrists' recommendations on another child and the effects were even more horrifying—when they gave him love and affection in response to his self-mutilation, he did it more. Within ten minutes he hit himself over two hundred times. Of course they immediately stopped the "recommended treatment"; the program could have killed him. It is obvious that for these two children, therapists' reassurance was a powerful reward—it encouraged their self-injurious behavior.

Since the publication of Lovaas' account of these cases in 1965, other therapists have noticed the same thing happen with other disturbed children. Well-meaning parents and relatives have actually made children become more self-destructive by giving them love and affection at the wrong time. Although the natural inclination for us all might be to comfort a child when he seems so upset, these cases demonstrate how misguided this reaction can sometimes be. As with a child who has tantrums, the disturbed child should receive love and affection when he's acting normally, not when he is abusing himself.

Timeout is one procedure that has worked. In the case of the three-and-a-half-year-old Dicky who wouldn't wear his glasses, isolation in a quiet room helped to eliminate his tantrums. However, this procedure has certain serious drawbacks when used with self-destructive children. Because it has to be repeated many times before the child actually ceases the problem behavior, the child might inflict serious injury before the treatment has an effect.

Thus, in cases when the child engages in self-destructive behavior, punishment may be the only way out. The reason that psychotherapists turn to this procedure is that it works— and it works fast. If the punishment is strong, it takes only a few experiences to eliminate the behavior. The punishment used with self-destructive children has been in the form of a brief (one-second) electric shock applied to the arm or leg. Although the shock is extremely unpleasant, like touching a faulty electric cord, the pain stops as soon as the shock is turned off, and it is physically harmless. In most instances the shock is delivered from a rigid metal tube filled with batteries. It works like a long flashlight with two electrodes at one end.

As soon as the child starts to harm himself, the therapist

touches the child's arm or leg with the rod. And the child instantly stops what he is doing. The effect is immediate. After only four or five experiences with the punishment, the self-injurious behavior ceases. During this therapy the child receives lots of love, praise and attention from the therapist when he is *not* engaging in the harmful behavior. Punishment is *never* used alone, but always in conjunction with abundant positive reinforcement. Lovaas and his co-workers never seem to be at all inhibited in expressing their warm feelings for the children, and often hug them affectionately when they do well.

On the surface it may seem almost inhuman to punish these severely disturbed children. But the only other alternatives are to let them go on injuring themselves, which obviously no one would want to do, or to keep them drugged or strait-jacketed for life, with no hope at all for improvement. When one considers that after only a few relatively harmless shocks the self-injurious behavior stops occurring and that the child can then go on to be trained to behave more appropriately in other areas, it becomes clear that this treatment is far more humane than any other now available.

The fear that many had concerning the children's reaction to punishment has not been supported. Rather than avoiding the therapists after they use punishment, the children seem to favor them—smiling and running to the therapists when they appear.

Since 1964 Lovaas and his colleagues have observed improvement with every single child they have treated, without exception. Inappropriate types of behavior such as bizarre speech and self-injury have decreased, and appropriate ones increased. As a result of treatment, these children have made substantial gains on standardized intelligence tests. They have also shown improvement in their interaction with others—they have become more outgoing and responsive to other people rather than being frantic and distraught.

In 1973, nine years after Lovaas began his work with disturbed children, he and his colleagues made a careful study of how the first twenty children had done since treatment.

They found considerable variation in the children's progress. Some of the children have continued to improve and others have not. Children who live with their parents at home have done the best, while children placed in large mental institutions regressed. The most disappointing case that Lovaas treated was a boy named Jose. At the beginning of therapy, when Jose was four, Lovaas characterized him as extremely negative. He was stubborn and withdrawn; he would bite himself and did not play with other children; he could not speak, wasn't toilet-trained and did not dress himself. After one year of behavior therapy he showed only moderate improvement. True, he became more interested in others, and would smile and respond to verbal directions, but he had a very limited vocabulary and was only partially toilet-trained. When they observed him in 1973, he was still quite disturbed. Although he is now toilet-trained and can feed himself, he is still very withdrawn and can use only a few words. Jose now attends a school for the mentally retarded.

Lovaas' greatest success was a child who entered their program at age four and a half, unable to talk or care for himself. Scottie was not interested in others and spent most of his time engaged in repetitive, stereotyped movements. During treatment he made fantastic progress and is at present attending a regular third grade. In Lovaas' words, Scottie "shows no trace of autism, and in all aspects must be considered a normal child."[4]

Although behaviorally oriented psychologists have done more for severely disturbed children than any other group of professionals has, they are not convinced that they have the whole answer. When gains have been made, there have been incredible amounts of time and effort devoted to each child. In Lovaas' project, each child received eight hours of treatment per day, six or seven days a week. And for those children who did best in this program, treatment did not end when the child left the hospital. Parents received extensive training and a great deal of assistance in working with their children. Lovaas and his colleagues are realistic in the evaluation of their program:

So far as we know, despite its limitations, it is the only intervention that is effective. Our program did not give everything to every child. Sometimes it gave very little to a particular child, but it did give something to each child we saw. The improvement was analogous to making from 10 to 20 steps on a 100-step ladder. Scotty probably started at 80 and gained 20; his treatment brought dramatic changes, he became normal and his change is irreversible. Jose, on the other hand, may have started at 10 and gained 10; the change was not all that dramatic.[5]

But for parents, even 10 to 20 steps represent gigantic leaps after years of frustration and anguish over their children's condition.

For severely disturbed adults the ladder also has 100 steps and the climb is equally arduous. Behavior modification has by no means offered a complete cure for these people, but it has proven to be the best method available.

Most psychologists have found that disturbed individuals are better off when they live at home and are treated on an outpatient basis. Behaviorists believe that this is because the "normal" environment provides more stimulation and better contingencies of reinforcement than the typical mental institution. When the disturbed individual lives at home he is usually required to meet the normal demands of daily living—being dressed, sociable, coherent and responsible—whereas on a large psychiatric ward the patient is allowed to literally sit, doing nothing. There is little stimulation. In many institutions, the only time the patient sees a professional is the day he is admitted and when the doctor comes around to increase his medication. What is more, he lacks those relationships that are most meaningful to him. But unfortunately, most disturbed adults must reside in some type of institution, either a psychiatric hospital or a shelter-care facility like a nursing home. Our society is intolerant of deviancy—regardless of how harmless. If someone looks strange, people are afraid and want to lock him up. It is also difficult for most disturbed people to live in the community because our mental-health system has failed to provide adequate community services. For example, even parents of young mentally retarded children often cannot find a dentist who will treat their children. In many large cities a person might have to travel two hours on public transportation to receive any treatment. Thus, while the ideal would be to carry out behavioral treatment programs within the real world of the community, most programs are found within psychiatric hospitals.

We should re-emphasize here that the kind of behavior modification we are discussing does not include psychosurgery and the implantation of electrodes in people's heads. In theory, behavior modification programs for disturbed adults incorporate the same principles that Dr. Jones used with Eleanor. The therapist identifies the problem behavior and devises procedures so that more adaptive types of behavior are reinforced and maladaptive behavior patterns are discouraged. Of course, it is a lot more difficult working with psychotic patients than well-educated neurotics. The problems of disturbed individuals are often much more difficult to understand and the patients are not always able to help in the therapy.

In most large behavior modification programs, certain objectives are applied to all patients. Since the ultimate goal is to make the patients able to lead productive lives outside the hospital, there is great emphasis on developing adequate communication, self-help and work skills. In almost all programs, patients receive rewards for coherent speech, good grooming and vocational competency. Patients receive training in these skills in specific classes and in one-to-one treatment through their day. If, for example, an extremely regressed person had difficulty organizing his personal possessions, a staff member would teach him how to set up his living area and then reward him when he does. Another person might receive special training in assertiveness. To make his job training really functional, training is focused on occupations where there are jobs. Often the staff finds a job in the community that will be available when the patient is discharged, and then directs at least part of the patient's training toward that particular job.

A particularly impressive example is a program that was directed by psychologist Gordon L. Paul of the University of Illinois. The program, conducted on Paul's Social Learning Unit in Decatur, was set up with funds from the National Institutes of Mental Health and the Illinois Department of Mental Health in 1968 as part of a six-year project designed to compare different methods of treatment at various hospitals. The unit housed 28 chronic mental patients at any one time, 14 men and 14 women, ranging in age from eighteen to fifty-five. They had been in state mental hospitals for years—the average length of hospitalization was seventeen years. Before the program began, all of them lived on hospital wards where they spent their days just sitting, being controlled by drugs. Many were incontinent and none of them were able to care for themselves. What is more, many of the patients were violent. And all were considered unsuited for community placement. They displayed many of the disturbed types of behavior we described earlier—disorganized thinking, bizarre movements and apathy—but were more disabled than any group of patients systematically treated before. The goal of the Social Learning Unit was to prepare these patients for living outside of psychiatric institutions.

Therapy and training were carried out round the clock. If a patient did not know how to shave, he was carefully taught how to use a razor; patients who did not dress themselves were taught to do so. And each step they made in learning earned them a reward. As a patient improved he received more opportunities and privileges, until by the time he had the necessary skills to be discharged he was familiar with the world outside the hospital. In addition to specific training in personal care and hygiene, patients attended both communication and basic arithmetic classes. Of course, treatment also involved social-skill training. As patients progressed they were given vocational training—how to fill out an application, how to go on a job interview, and for those who were to live independently, how to do a specific type of work.

To help maintain the gains made in the program, the staff

made sure that each released patient had social support in the community—a relative or friend responsible for providing social companionship or a board-and-room placement where social support was available.

In order to evaluate the effectiveness of the program, the therapists conducted continuous monitoring of each patient's functioning, as well as special assessments every six months. They compared their results with the progress made by similar patients treated by traditional mental-hospital procedures.

The Social Learning Program was more effective than the other programs. A typical example of improvement is the case of Bobbi F., a fifty-two-year-old former housewife. She had been hospitalized for the past fourteen years, much of that time in back wards where she had been restrained in hydrotherapy tubs. When she was observed before being admitted to the Social Learning Unit, she was running around the hospital ward nude, climbing over the furniture. During the week before entering the unit, she made twenty-three physical assaults on staff members and other patients. She also appeared to be hallucinating, often shouting things like "There is a vampire on the wall" and "They are going to kill Princess Grace." In terms of appropriate behavior, such as bathing, maintaining her personal appearance and interacting with others, she was totally deficient.

After only eighteen weeks in the Social Learning Program, her assaults on others had diminished to less than one incident a week, and her delusional statements had all but disappeared. Furthermore, she had developed many appropriate types of behavior that she had totally lacked before the treatment. By the end of two years, in the words of Paul, "Bobbi had literally changed from functioning as a savage animal to a pleasant human being, with quite a sense of humor."[6] After being discharged from the unit, Bobbi moved into a private boarding-house facility in the community. At the time Paul made his final report, Bobbi had been living in the community for over one year.

The other patients in the Social Learning Program

showed similar improvement, and all of them achieved release from the institution. On the other hand, fewer than half of the patients who remained in traditional treatment were able to leave the institution. From Paul's research it can be concluded that compared to other methods, treatment based on social-learning principles clearly emerges as the treatment of choice for the chronically institutionalized mental patient.

Almost no word adequately describes the tragic plight of psychotic individuals. As yet, no cure for them has been found. But behavior therapy has helped many previously hopeless individuals get out of the back wards and become marginally functioning human beings. It is not a cure, but it is a real achievement by any standards.

In the Classroom

Children learn best if they enjoy it. But it is at this crucial and fundamental level that our schools fail miserably. Even in communities where violence is not a problem, research studies have shown that unpleasantness and hostility characterize many public-school classrooms. From a survey of teachers conducted in 1970, University of Florida Professor C. H. Madsen and his colleagues reported that 77 percent of the interactions between teachers and students were negative. This situation becomes worse in later grades. In a recent study (December 1975) Professor Mary White of Columbia Teachers College reported observations of both urban and suburban schools. The results are most disturbing. In every grade after the second, negative comments from teachers exceeded positive. The reason for this unfortunate state of affairs should by now be familiar. As in other situations we've examined, it is only natural that when things are going smoothly, and the students are working quietly at their desks or are absorbed in a project at the back of the room, the teacher is not going to shower them with praise and attention. He will use the time instead to get some of his chores done at his desk, or concentrate on other students. It is when things are *not* going smoothly, and students are rambunctiously tossing pocket calculators out the window and shredding textbooks, while learning very little, that attention from the teacher, of one sort or another, is going to come.

Not only does this way of interacting give the teacher the frustrating feeling that his role is primarily a disciplinary one, but it does not achieve the goal of a well-run classroom. Rather than eliminating the children's misbehavior, the teacher's reactions often encourage it. In the context of a busy classroom where children may go unrecognized for periods of time, it is not surprising that attention from the teacher, even if it is negative, acts as a reinforcer. And so, unintentional though it may be, the teacher ends up encouraging the students' bad behavior.

To improve the way teachers deal with students, behavior modification—which is now routinely taught in most university teacher training programs—emphasizes the effective use of positive reinforcement and timeout. In a pioneer project carried out in a public elementary school in Urbana, Illinois, psychologist Wesley Becker and his associates taught specific behavior-modification techniques to teachers. At the completion of the seminar series, teachers were asked to keep a 5 × 8 index card summarizing the techniques on the corner of their desks as a reminder of the new methods. The card contained three principles to follow:

1. Make explicit rules as to what is expected of children for each period. (Remind of rules when needed.)
2. *Ignore* (do not attend to) behaviors which interfere with learning or teaching, unless a child is being hurt by another. Use punishment which seems appropriate, preferably withdrawal of some positive reinforcement.
3. Give *praise* and *attention* to behaviors which facilitate learning. Tell child what he is being praised for. Try to reinforce

behaviors incompatible with those you wish to decrease. Examples of how to praise: "I like the way you're working quietly." "That's the way I like to see you work." "Good job, you're doing fine." Transition period. "I see Johnny is ready to work." "I'm calling on you because you raised your hand." "I wish everyone were working as nicely as X." etc. Use variety and expression.

In general, give praise for achievement, prosocial behavior and following the group rules.[1]

To evaluate the effectiveness of their training program, Becker and his staff selected ten of the most disruptive children from five different classes and carefully observed them. Before the program began they saw them doing such things as hitting and pinching other children, damaging books and classroom equipment and disturbing the class by talking out of turn, tapping their feet or banging pencils on their desks. During observation made before the program began the ten children were disruptive 62 percent of the time.

To give an idea of exactly what happened we will quote directly from the report. We have selected one child who is representative of the ten children who were observed. He was a seven-and-a-half-year-old boy named Albert. Although his scores on the Stanford-Binet Intelligence Test were normal, he was approximately one year behind in school. Becker selected him for the study because he showed many types of behavior which interfered with his learning. Mrs. A, his teacher, described how he behaved before the program began:

> He was a very noisy, disruptive child. He fought with others, blurted out, could not stay in his seat, and did very little required work. I had to check constantly to see that the minimum work was finished. He sulked and responded negatively to everything suggested to him. In addition, he was certain that he could not read. If I had planned it, I could not have reinforced this negative behavior more, for I caught him in every deviant act possible and often before it occurred. I lectured him

and, as might be expected, was making only backward motion. In November Albert came to me to tell me something and I was shocked by the intensity of his stuttering. He simply could not express his thought because his stuttering was so bad.[2]

After she started using the techniques Mrs. A reported:

He quickly responded and his deviant behavior decreased to 10%, the lowest recorded. Along with the praising and ignoring, I attempted to establish a calmer atmosphere in which to work, and carefully reviewed class behavior rules. A good technique with Albert was to have him repeat the rule because "he was following it."[3]

Albert's disruptive behavior dropped to an average of 8 percent as a result of the program. However, Mrs. A noticed that Albert was not as well behaved when her student teacher took charge of the class. Mrs. A reported:

As my student teacher gradually assumed more and more of the teaching load, the deviant behavior increased again. She made the same mistakes that I had. Gradually, she accepted the positive approach and in the last week or two of her work the deviant behavior began again to decrease. She had learned that with so negative a child as Albert, only building rapport by using positive reinforcement would succeed.

Albert has improved delightfully. He still blurts out, but makes an effort to stop this. He is often seen holding his hand in the air biting his lips. He completes his work on time, and it is done well. Often, when he has to re-do a paper, he takes it cheerfully and says, "I can do this myself." No sulking. He still finds it difficult to sit for a long period of time, but time on task has increased. He works very hard on his reading and has stated that he can read. His stuttering has decreased almost to zero. When the observers were questioned concerning this, they had detected little, if any stuttering. Most important to me, Albert has become a delightful child and an enthusiastic member of our class who feels his ideas are accepted and have merit.[4]

The program was equally effective for the other children. Within less than nine weeks, the average percent of deviant behavior decreased 33 percent from the level that existed before the training program was implemented.

Since this seminal study, other psychologists and educators have improved on the techniques. One major development has been the proliferation of what behaviorists call *token economies in classrooms.* In such systems the teacher rewards the children with plastic chips or some type of point (i.e., tokens) that can be exchanged for treats and special privileges. Like in any other behavior-modification program, the teacher carefully explains the token system to the children so that they know what is expected of them and how to earn tokens.

The rules for receiving tokens vary from class to class and usually from child to child. In the ideal situation the requirements for reinforcement depend upon the individual child's level of ability. If, for example, George has trouble with arithmetic and takes a long time doing each problem, then the teacher would set his work requirements much lower than for Anne, who is a whiz with numbers. Two problems might earn George a token, whereas his classmate would need ten problems. The idea is to motivate all the children to work at their best, regardless of their ability level. George might have to work all day to do ten problems and would most likely be discouraged before he earned his first token. Yet, if Anne, who is good at math, had the same reinforcement requirements as George, she would get tokens so fast that she might become satiated and stop trying. With a flexible system like this, it is assumed that both children will experience success, yet be challenged at the same time.

With their tokens the children purchase their rewards. At some later time (perhaps later that day) the children trade in their chips for goodies at a canteen set up in the classroom. To make sure that each child is motivated, the teacher keeps the store well stocked with their favorite treats: candy, small games and toys. Tickets for special events such as field trips and movies are sometimes made available. Each child should find things that he likes and wants and will work for. Since all children don't necessarily like the same things, the stock is usually quite varied. In some classrooms the children decide how the store is stocked. Ellen might be saving her tokens for a baseball, and Mary might want a coloring book. Children can also decide on a large item and save up their tokens to buy it. But the system must be individualized to respond to the needs and preferences of all the children.

The effectiveness of a token system can be readily determined: just look at the children's progress. If a child is not improving, then something has got to change. Either the reinforcement requirements are too easy or too hard, or the items in the store are too expensive, too cheap or no longer interesting. (As in our society, recession, depression and inflation affect the children's behavior.) The teacher must adopt some of the characteristics of an economic analyst and tailor the work experience to each child's needs.

Token economies may bring about a lot of changes in the classroom. For one thing, a pocketful of tokens is a good reminder for the teacher to use positive reinforcement. (This phenomenon was recently observed by psychologists Norman Breyer and George Allen of the University of Connecticut. They found that the rate of positive comments from the teachers increased dramatically, and negative comments decreased, when they instituted a token system.) Furthermore, since the teacher has to pay close attention to each child in order to know when the tokens should be given, the system ensures greater teacher attention. Even if the teacher sometimes overlooks a child's accomplishments, the child will not forget— "Mr. Doran, I finished my workbook" or "I improved in reading today." This type of system involves more work for the teacher but provides a gratifying sense of accomplishment. What's more, teachers have found that kids love it and their work improves. As secondary benefit, token systems give children experience in dealing with a monetary system. Some classrooms even have banks that pay interest for saving.

Token systems are not intended to replace close personal interaction and rapport between the teacher and the students.

Rather, they usually result in increased communication and a more rewarding experience for students and teachers alike.

But isn't this just bribery? Instead of being motivated by the rather crass and materialistic desire to collect chips and trade them in for possessions, "things" or amusements, shouldn't children in school want to do well because of their interest in the information and their love of learning?

Most psychologists would agree that that is the ideal motivation, and as we shall see, much work is being done in curriculum development to make learning rewarding in itself. Still, children, like the rest of us, often require extra encouragement. And they have never been without some incentive besides the work itself to get them to apply themselves and behave well in school. In days past, teachers came equipped with a birch rod; today they use grades. Token economies are no closer to bribery than these other systems. The word "bribery," after all, implies corruption; one does not speak of "bribing" the teacher with money to make him teach his students. Many educators, in fact, have argued that token reinforcement systems are *more* ethical than the more familiar methods because they avoid the punitive atmosphere of many traditional classrooms.

There has also been a remarkable improvement in many special classrooms where token reinforcement has been used. In one class for emotionally disturbed children, the amount of time the children actually spent occupied in school-related activities increased two and a half times as their behavior improved. Some impressive statistics come from a classroom of poor readers in fifth and sixth grades in Lawrence, Kansas. These children showed twice as much progress as a group of similar children who remained in a regular classroom. Their scores on a standardized achievement test increased an amount equivalent to one and a half years over a period of nine months. Moreover, their grades went up more than one letter.

Behavioral programs have produced similar results with economically disadvantaged children. The best-known programs are two models funded by the U.S. Office of Education's Project Follow-Through. Follow-Through is an experimental project with the goal of discovering ways to help these children do better in school, and stems from the heavily funded Head Start Program. Head Start is aimed to help disadvantaged children prepare for many aspects of the classroom situation with which they are unfamiliar. Children are selected on a monetary basis: if the family income falls below the poverty level, they can be enrolled in the special preschool program. Although there is wide variation in what is taught in different Head Start classrooms, the major emphasis is on teaching skills considered to be prerequisites for academic learning. The schools expose the children to reading and math concepts, take them on field trips and give them many of the enriching experiences familiar to children from more affluent families. But when studies were conducted to evaluate Head Start, it became apparent that the initial improvement in the children's academic performance evaporated by the time they had been in elementary school for a year or two. Many of them were doing no better than children who had not been in Head Start. In order to prevent the children's falling behind, the federal government instituted Project Follow-Through.

Twenty-five projects received funds to try out different approaches. Two of them, the Engelman-Becker Program and the Behavior Analysis Program sponsored by Professor Don Bushell, use behavior modification. One program uses a strict token economy and provides materials, such as workbooks, that are designed to allow children to work at their own pace. In the other program, teachers concentrate on rewarding "working hard" and skill acquisition in daily teaching sessions. In both programs, teachers are encouraged to keep in close touch with the progress of each student; as many as two aides per classroom may be trained to help the teacher give each child immediate feedback and frequent reinforcement.

The final evaluation of the twenty-five Follow-Through models has not yet been made, but an interim report in 1972 showed that the behaviorally based programs were ranked as the most successful (first and second highest). The third-grade children in the Engelman-Becker Program were reading fluently at a high fourth-grade level rather than at mid-second-grade level, which is the expected reading achievement for these children. Results like these give a powerful boost to the idea that behavior modification can really help kids learn.

Still, there is considerable controversy about what behavior modification is used for in many classrooms. The real goals of certain programs are rather questionable. If the children only get rewards for things like "sitting at your desk" and "not talking" (as, indeed, they have been in some programs), then it seems as though the teacher is benefiting from the program, but not the students. Behaviorists are capable of providing teachers with classrooms of students who stay rooted to their desks and never talk out of turn, and that is what some teachers want. But the question is, Is that the best way to help children learn? Not necessarily.

As many behaviorists are ashamed to admit, behavior modification has been used as a tool of the status quo for the maintenance of law and order in the classroom. Psychologist Richard Winett and Robin Winkler quite poignantly pointed out this fact in a paper entitled "Current Behavior Modification in the Classroom: Be Still, Be Quiet, Be Docile." They argued that in far too many instances the behavioral goals relate only to the comfort of the teacher, without any consideration given to the intellectual improvement of the students. What kinds of things are being reinforced? they ask. Reviewing the reports published in the most widely read journal in the area (the *Journal of Applied Behavior Analysis*), the authors find a distressing list of objectives—the elimination of inappropriate behavior, including

> getting out of seat, standing up, walking around, running, hopping, skipping, jumping, moving chairs, rocking chairs, tapping feet, rattling papers, carrying on a conversation with other children, crying, singing, whistling, laughing, turning head or body toward another child, and looking at another child.

Appropriate behavior included

> attending to the teacher, raising hand and waiting for the teacher to respond, working in seat on a workbook, following in a reading text.[5]

They end by adding to the list of behavior to be eliminated: "doing something different from that which he has been directed to do, or is supposed to do."[6]

Although Winett and Winkler's observations have generally been accepted as valid, they have been criticized for exaggerating the problem and ignoring a large number of projects which, in fact, have focused on teaching skills—reading performance, accuracy in arithmetic—that are clearly related to learning. We must also recognize that these abuses of behavior modification are clearly that, a misuse of the methods. The problem lies not with the techniques themselves, but with the people who used the technique.

A review of the recent literature on behavior modification in education shows a decided shift in emphasis away from "classroom deportment" toward more complex processes. Behaviorists are now focusing on things like creativity and problem solving in young children.

Another behavioral approach emphasizes that not only should a child be generously rewarded for his accomplishments, he should not be frustrated. Learning ought to be easy and free of errors. To make this possible, some behavioral specialists have devised what is called *programmed learning,* or individualized instruction. They break down the material to be learned into small units, which are then carefully put in order so that each lesson builds on the work that has come before. The student is shown some material which he is to learn; then he must do something with it, such as selecting and pressing the correct buttons to answer questions, or typing the answers on a special computer typewriter. Or he may simply write, read aloud or point to a word or numeral or picture. If he responds correctly, he gets positive feedback—perhaps the teacher says "Good reading! That's right, go on!" or the computer prints out "Great! Push button 'E' to go on." If the student does not answer correctly, he may be directed to go back and review, or to work on additional material to help him learn better. If a student answers all the questions correctly without any studying, he can skip ahead to more challenging material. This method permits each student to move at his own pace. No one has to fall behind, and students needn't get bored while waiting for slower students to catch up.

So far, individualized instruction programs have been developed for teaching everyone from mentally retarded children through students in college and medical school. Computer technology has made possible the development of whole "libraries" of programmed courses of instruction. At the University of Illinois, for instance, 300 different courses are available in the PLATO system. With computer terminals located throughout the world, over 4,000 hours of programmed lessons are available to serve students at all levels. In one fifth-grade classroom PLATO was so popular that the children actually hurried to finish other assignments in order to use it, and even voluntarily stayed after school to work with the machine.

The most revolutionary impact of this notion that teaching should be geared to the individual has been in the education of mentally retarded children. If, as has always been the common practice, a child is written off as being too handicapped to learn and then is treated that way, then he's not likely to make much progress. But by making the assumption that anyone can learn if he is taught in a way that is right for him, behaviorists have improved the lives of the mentally retarded. These children can and do learn if teaching is geared to their needs and deficits. When someone has difficulty learning a particular concept or skill, the behaviorist believes that something is wrong with the way he is being taught, and that the method should be changed to fit his needs. A behavior modifier will not give up on a child because the child "doesn't get it" or isn't smart enough, so these children are now learning more than was ever believed possible.

Not only are behavioral psychologists and educators developing special programs for the retarded but they are also training teachers to devise their own programs. The steps that the teachers must follow are similar to those we have described earlier—assessment, gradual progression through skill training, and so on. The teacher begins by making a careful assessment of each child's ability, and then sequences the teaching materials so that there is a gradual and logical progression from the child's current level to the desired goal.

In order for teachers to know at what level to begin teaching, they must know "where" the child is. For instance, before he can train a mute child to speak, the teacher must know what skills he has that are relevant to speaking. Can the child hear? Will the child imitate sounds that he hears? Follow verbal instructions? Express his wishes with gestures? Answers to questions like these tell the teacher exactly where to begin.

Educators have traditionally felt that knowledge of the child's I.Q. would help them in working with the child. However, there is a growing disenchantment with this type of information, and many professionals have found I.Q. scores of little practical value. The speed with which the child completes a puzzle or copies a block design on an I.Q. test does not tell the teacher what skills should be taught first. Many behaviorists also feel that information regarding the child's I.Q. may do more harm than good. As soon as people find out that a child has a low I.Q., they often assume that he cannot learn much, and will not expect him to. To avoid this prejudice, many teachers and psychologists do not even want to have that information. They want to know what specific things the child does that will help him acquire a particular skill.

To see how a behavioral training program might be set up, we can focus on a self-feeding program for a severely retarded child. Before starting the program, the teacher observes him eating a meal at the table. Most likely he's grabbing food with both hands and stuffing it into his mouth, spilling some and messing his face and clothing, the table and the floor. Spoon and fork remain on the table, unused. Or perhaps, to prevent a mess, someone is spoon-feeding the child.

At the next meal the teacher sits near the child and physically helps him through the motions of eating. She places a spoon in the child's hand, guides him through the task of filling it with food and then bringing it up and into his mouth. The child consumes the spoonful of food and the process is repeated. Once the training program has begun, the teacher never allows him to stuff food into his mouth with his fingers. The teacher repeats the process with every bit of food. When the child becomes more comfortable with the task, the teacher gradually removes her help. She might begin by releasing her hand as the child gets the spoon to his lips, and if he succeeds in getting it into his mouth without her help she fades out another part of her assistance. As the training progresses she gradually withdraws all her help, until finally the child is entirely on his own. (This training process is much like the way one teaches a child to ride a bike—at first one gives complete support and guidance. As the child becomes able to balance himself, the support is gradually removed, almost without the child's realizing it.) If the child experiences any difficulty along the way, the teacher is ready to step in and give the needed assistance. As with all behavior-modification programs, teaching is individualized to the capabilities of each student.

There are now published programs for teaching both social and academic skills to mentally retarded individuals, regardless of their deficits. These developments represent a radical change in the methods used to treat the mentally retarded. Traditionally these people have lived in large state institutions called schools. These facilities, though located in remote areas with plenty of sunshine and fresh air, lacked stimulation. Housed in warehouselike dormitories, the children spent most of their time just sitting. Since they were presumed to be hopeless, not much money was spent on education and entertainment. Nurses and attendants saw to it that they were dressed, fed and put to bed—the retarded person was not responsible for anything because, of course, he was *incompe-*

tent. So much was done for these people that there was no reason for them to learn how to do anything for themselves. And since they were unstimulated, they became passive. These procedures actually worsened the problems of the patients. They were mentally retarded individuals placed in "retarding" environments. Just imagine how you might behave in a situation in which you had virtually nothing to do for years on end. To foster the development of the patients, the institution would have to change how patients were treated. For behavior modifiers, that meant providing stimulation for patients, and rewarding individuals less for passivity and compliance, and more for the kind of behavior which is expected outside the institution. In a very real sense, this training meant giving the mentally retarded the advantages of a normal environment.

To make this kind of treatment available to the majority of retarded people, we would have to change the physical, social and educational structure of our institutions. The Scandinavians were the first to implement these notions on a large scale by closing many of their large custodial institutions and replacing them with smaller facilities located in middle-class neighborhoods. The residents usually have private rooms, their own money, and are responsible for themselves. As much as possible, the supervisory staff keeps out of sight and intervenes only in emergencies. Even with the more severely retarded, the trend is toward small facilities and structured activities scheduled throughout the day. The goal has been to provide these individuals as normal an environment as possible. And now this trend has begun to appear in the United States as well.

This notion that the mentally retarded child is better off in a normal environment has also affected families with retarded children. Twenty years ago a kindly physician would have advised parents to place their retarded child in an institution where he could receive good *care.* Today the doctor would more likely refer them to a special educator or psychologist who will advise parents how best to encourage their child's development. The public-school system in Portage, Wisconsin, has even set up a parent-training program for this exact purpose.

Run by two behaviorally oriented teachers, David and Marsha Shearer, the program trains parents of handicapped children to teach effectively. Depending upon the age and ability of the child, parents learn how to teach self-help and pre-academic skills. Teachers also demonstrate the use of behavioral techniques and discuss issues that the parents feel are important. All of the parent training is carried out in the home, with the teacher first demonstrating and then observing the parents as they work with their child. Parents also receive reading material and workbooks to supplement the teacher's instruction. The Portage Project has been in operation since 1972 and preliminary evaluation indicated that the program is achieving its goal. The children are progressing about 25 percent faster than would otherwise have been expected. Parents report that they have also benefited from the program. Not only can they handle their retarded child better, they find that they are more effective with their other children. The parents also feel proud of their ability to help their child in a meaningful way.

There is no denying that our educational institutions are in deep trouble. Many children are not learning how to read and write, and classrooms all over the country are beset by violence of a ferocity that was unimaginable only a few years ago. The behavior-modification programs we have examined in this chapter may be a significant first step toward solving these major problems. They have been successful both in improving classroom behavior and in presenting material in ways that make children want to learn. We are not suggesting that knife-wielding sixth graders are going to be miraculously tamed by M & M candies and teaching machines overnight. But remember the unruly California boys who learned to make use of behavioral principles to get along better with their teachers. Applied with imagination, energy and care, behavior modification will undoubtedly be a powerful asset in the struggle to make our schools the effective institutions our society so desperately needs.

X

Behavior Modification Used against People

There are also horror stories. Though behavior modification is far from the point of enabling a master controller to make us all into compliant subjects, it *has* been used as a means of domineering helpless people. During the last five years there have been seven major court decisions regarding the constitutionality of behavior-modification programs. The most serious abuses have been those perpetrated against people who have little chance of fighting back—institutionalized mental patients and prison inmates.

Civil libertarians have brought two charges against behavior-modification programs for rehabilitating prisoners—one is the failure of prison officials to secure the consent of the inmates participating in the programs, and the other is the use of cruel and unusual punishment. In almost all of the prison programs the inmates have been forced into receiving treatment. They are not given a real choice. Even if their consent is requested, some institutional review committees have later denied the inmates the right to refuse. For example, in the prison hospital at Vacaville, California, five prisoners refused to enter a "conditioning" treatment program that involved a drug causing the temporary sensation of suffocation and loss of muscle control. After considering the program and the inmates' refusals to participate, the institution's review board reversed the inmates' decisions and enrolled them in the program.

Even when prisoners agree to participate "voluntarily," coercion is, nevertheless, a distinct possibility. Promises of early release often accompany requests for inmate participation, and parole boards usually look favorably on inmates who cooperate in treatment programs. Even without explicit promises, the prisoner's incarceration may make him feel coerced. In a survey reported by psychologist Robert E. Kennedy of the Pennsylvania State University, it was found that 77 percent of those participating in one therapy program claimed that they did so solely to impress their parole board.

Another criticism is that many of the methods are nothing more than sophisticated torture. In one program, prison officials injected inmates with vomit-inducing drugs as punishment for offenses such as swearing and not getting out of bed. Many behavior modifiers agree that such procedures do, indeed, constitute cruel and exorbitant punishment, particularly since many of the "aversive" techniques used are not effective and therefore not therapeutic, besides being unethical and repugnant.

Even where prison programs have not employed brutal punishment, authorities are extremely critical. They claim that in many instances "recommended" behavioral practices (i.e., careful assessment of the conditions associated with a person's problems, individualization of treatment programs, continuous evaluation of each person's progress, and total client participation in devising the program) have not been followed. That is, many of the prison rehabilitation programs do not represent "good" behavior modification. Because of the extremely restrictive policies of most prisons, it is doubtful whether "ethical" behavior modification is even possible in our present penal system.

The legal and ethical issues concerning behavior modification are exceedingly complex. In an effort to resolve some of these issues, the Institute for Behavioral Research in Bethesda, Maryland, has established the Behavioral Law Center. Its purpose is to establish mechanisms for behavioral psychologists and lawyers to use in devising effective therapeutic practices that do not violate individual rights.

The classic portrayal of the brutal use of behavior-modification techniques is Anthony Burgess's tale of *A Clockwork Orange*. In the book, the police arrest Alex, a young hoodlum who has been the ringleader in a series of savage and sadistic attacks on innocent citizens. He is taken to a prison hospital for treatment and strapped down in a theater seat with his eyelids pinned open. After receiving an injection that quickly creates feelings of panic and extreme nausea, he is forced to watch films of violence. The idea is that if he learns to associate acts of violence with the horrifying sensations created by the medication, then he will stop engaging in vicious crimes. Within a few treatment sessions, Alex is "cured" and the mere thought of violence evokes extreme anxiety. He has been made docile.

Horrifyingly enough, Burgess's prediction has already come true, with startling accuracy. The only difference between his science fiction and reality is that the methods do not turn out to be as effective as they were portrayed in the book.

An early application of such techniques was in the prison hospital in Vacaville, California, in 1970. The goal was to eliminate antisocial behavior in inmates who failed to get along in the prison. They were guilty of such things as fighting, deviant sexual behavior and failing to cooperate in group psychotherapy. The treatment followed the lines described by Burgess. The prisoner was given Anectine, a derivative of the poison curare. As the drug takes effect a sensation of numbness moves throughout the body, and then an incapacitating paralysis strikes. The subject cannot move his limbs or hold up his head. And for one or two minutes his diaphragm stops pumping—he is unable to breathe. According to Dr. Arthur Nugent, chief psychiatrist at Vacaville, the prisoner experiences the terrifying feeling of being on the brink of death. When the inmate begins having sensations of suffocation and drowning, the therapist, in a cold and unsympathetic voice, tells him to think about his antisocial behavior and to remember the terrifying sensation of suffocation. Just before the effects diminish, the therapist reminds the inmate that the treatment will be repeated if he continues to transgress. According to Dr. Nugent, "Even the toughest inmates have come to fear and hate the drug. I don't blame them, I wouldn't have one treatment myself for the world." Neverless, as Jessica Mitford reported in *Harper's,* Dr. Nugent is an enthusiast for the treatment.[1]

For prisoners convicted of child molesting, two programs (one at the Connecticut State Prison in Somers, Connecticut, and the other at the prison in Atascadero, California) used electric shock applied to the groin area to eliminate the inmates' sexual responses to children. Similar to the technique of *A Clockwork Orange,* the pedophiles were shocked while viewing pictures of young children. Again, the idea was to make such acts repugnant by associating them with the pain of electric shock.

All of these programs have been terminated as the result of lawsuits brought by the prisoners. The courts have ruled that subjecting nonconsenting prisoners to programs involving the use of unproven treatment methods constituted a violation of the Eighth Amendment.

Even greater controversy has surrounded the proliferation of round-the-clock total-participation rehabilitation programs in federal and state penitentiaries. The most publicized was START (Special Treatment and Rehabilitation Training), established in 1972 at the Medical Center for Federal Prisoners in Springfield, Missouri. According to Dr. Robert B. Levinson of the Bureau of Prisons, the purpose of the program was to devise ways to manage the prison system's most disruptive and

aggressive inmates. These were prisoners whose extreme violence required their being segregated from other inmates and
kept in isolated cells. Prior to being admitted to the program,
eleven "participants" had committed serious offenses while in
prison. Six were guilty of murdering either guards or fellow
inmates. The aim of the program was not to prepare these men
for life outside the prison, but rather to help them gain better
control over their assaultive behavior so that they would be able
to function within the regular prison programs. START was
viewed by its originators as "prerehabilitatory" and as an alternative to the usual practice of "deadlocking" (i.e., solitary
confinement).

Admission to the program was involuntary, and was based
on a warden's recommendation plus a review by the program's
staff. START incorporated what is called a level system. Each
inmate would begin at the "orientation" level and then advance as he demonstrated "improvement." The orientation
level was similar to solitary confinement. The inmate was
locked in his 6' by 10' cell almost continuously; the only things
he had were a Bible and a hometown newspaper. He was
allowed to change his clothes and bathe only twice a week. He
had no radio, no cigarettes, and could not have visitors. As he
advanced, by being obedient and following orders with no
argument, his privileges were gradually increased until, at the
final level, all of the regular prison privileges were restored. He
could visit the library, have visitors, shower daily, etc. When
he reached the higher levels he would move to a point system
in which he was rewarded for personal appearance, could work
in the prison factory and progress in individualized learning
programs. He could also earn points for being cooperative and
obedient to the prison rules. Points were like money and could
be used at the prison commissary to rent such items as radios
and musical instruments.

Disobedience or noncooperation resulted in immediate
loss of all privileges and a return to solitary confinement. The
duration of this isolation varied, depending upon the will of the
staff. It often lasted for days.

From the reports that are available it is difficult to determine exactly how effective the program was. Authorities have presented conflicting data. In his address to the American Psychological Association, Dr. Levinson claimed "moderate" success—half of the inmates who entered the program progressed to the top level and were transferred back to regular prison programs. However, in a report filed in the U.S. District Court for the Western District of Missouri by attorney Arpiar G. Saunders, Jr., and his colleagues from the American Civil Liberties Union, a different conclusion was drawn: the program failed miserably. According to the latter report, five of the inmates were transferred to the prison's psychiatric hospital rather than to a regular ward, four were transferred out because they never moved beyond the first level, and two were released without completing the program. The other inmates were still in the program when it was terminated in February 1974. Even without trying to make order out of the conflicting reports, it is clear that the START program did not achieve the results that would be expected from a truly effective program.

The criticisms of the program come from all sides: civil libertarians, behaviorists and prison inmates. And like the *Clockwork Orange* abuses we described earlier, the objections concern problems of coercion, cruel and unusual punishment, and ill-conceived applications of behavioral principles. According to Professor Kennedy's report of prison projects, the highly coercive nature of the program not only infringed on the prisoners' constitutional rights, but also reduced the potential effectiveness of the program. Kennedy pointed out in his review of the therapy-for-prisoners controversy that mandatory participation in START tended to make the inmates view the entire program as punishment. They sought (and found) some means of retaliation. Seven of the prisoners staged a sixty-five-day hunger strike in protest against the program and subsequently sued the staff for violating their constitutional rights (*Clonce* v. *Richardson*, 1974). From the very beginning of the program the general atmosphere was one of "them against us." The fact that inmates had no role in planning their programs only heightened this feeling. Professor Harold L. Cohen, an expert witness in the START case, reported that the staff reacted negatively to any suggestions prisoners made, often threatening to remove privileges if they continued to complain. Although the original program proposal that received favorable review by behavorial psychologist Nate Azrin provided for individualized programs and contracts for earning points and privileges, no such programs or contracts were ever made.

The program was originally billed as a positive approach to dealing with the most difficult inmates, but careful observation of what really went on in the program suggests otherwise. For one thing, the prisoner's first encounter with the program, the orientation level, was aversive. Stripped of all his personal possessions and privileges, the prisoner had to work his way out of hell. Another negative facet of the program, uncovered in an ACLU investigation, was the excessive use of corporal punishment. Following his inspection of the facility on behalf of a group of inmates, ACLU attorney Saunders wrote a detailed letter describing the abuses he observed to Dr. Pasquale J. Ciccone, director of the Springfield penitentiary:

> In my recent visit to the Medical Center I was shocked to learn that two of the fifteen involuntary participants in the START program—[names withheld]—were shackled by their arms and legs by means of leather and metal straps and chains to their steel beds. Additionally, I learned that on several occasions in the five days they had been shackled (as of February 21st), they had been forced to eat with both hands still shackled to the bed and had experienced great difficulty in receiving staff assistance in removing the chains in order to perform necessary bodily functions. These conditions were particularly disturbing in light of the Federal Bureau of Prisons policy statement which had seemingly outlawed such cruel and inhuman punishment.
>
> Even more outrageous is the fact that neither individual was ever charged with or made an appearance before a disciplinary committee for violation of a rule or regulation. It appears that these two individuals were and continue to be subjected to cruel and arbitrary punishment.
>
> In addition to the two individuals noted above, four other

individuals—[names withheld]—have also been subjected to cruel and arbitrary treatment allegedly because of their non-cooperative attitude within the involuntary START program . . .

The punitive treatment that these six individuals have been and continue to be subjected to by your staff forces me to believe that the START program is but a medical sham, with the true objective of subjecting certain selected individuals to an experimental program which is simply cruel and unusual punishment inflicted on these individuals for their past behavior without regard to Federal Bureau of Prisons policies concerned with inmate discipline or the conditions, rules and regulations of segregation grade custody.[2]

Professor Cohen was similarly appalled by the brutality and agreed that the program was a sham. We quote from his address to the Association for the Advancement of Behavior Therapy Convention:

I did not consider it a sound behavior modification program. Some of my reasons were: they never elicited the participation of the inmates, they did not reasonably measure the responses they were supposedly to have been shaping, and there were no explicitly developed interpersonal or academic programs to help direct the men. Record keeping was never kept on educational behavior; and poorly kept on behavior; good record keeping was on the production of brooms. . . . I recommend to the courts to discontinue the programs.[3]

Regardless of whether or not such punishment can legitimately be called behavior modification, it clearly violates laws governing how prisoners can be treated.

One of the main aspects of the START program that has been criticized is its original goals. In obvious contradiction to the notion that the client should have a primary role in establishing treatment goals, the objectives of START were directed toward the comfort of the staff. Like the grade-school teacher

who wants a class full of docile, obedient children, the administration wanted to create meek and compliant inmates. According to Cohen, the attitude of the staff was "wait until the
subject submits and then begin to reinforce him." A brief
review of the rules for level advancement and the earning of
points makes staff intentions clear. In order to advance from
one level to another, the prisoner had to accrue a certain
number of "good days." The criteria of a "good day" included
accepting "no" as an answer without argument, accepting assigned duties without resistance, and following all rules and
regulations. Some of the transgressions that resulted in "solitary" and level demotion were excessive arguing, swearing and
disobeying a staff member. To succeed in START an inmate
had to become meek.

Given the men selected for the program, a more impossible goal could not have been conceived. These inmates were
the most aggressive individuals in the system; and access to a
radio or an extra ten minutes of exercise were hardly strong
enough incentives to get them to be submissive. Thus, it is not
surprising that the guards quickly turned to the technique they
knew best, punishment.

Some people might take issue with the criticism of the
goals of START. While they recognize that the program may
have violated certain constitutional rights, they argue that such
individuals deserve whatever they get. In essence they are
saying that an individual looses certain rights when he commits
a crime against others. University of Michigan psychology professor James V. McConnell, in his article "Criminals Can Be
Brainwashed—Now," has suggested that anyone who has been
convicted of committing a serious crime has, by so doing,
forfeited his civil rights and therefore can be legitimately subjected to treatment designed to alter his personality and behavior, regardless of his wishes.

> I don't believe the Constitution of the United States gives you
> the *right* to commit a crime if you want to; therefore, the
> Constitution does not guarantee you the right to maintain invi-

olable the personality it forced on you in the first place—if and
when the personality manifests strongly antisocial behavior.[4]

But constitutional authorities disagree, citing the First, Eighth
and Ninth Amendments.

Another issue posed in opposition to the heavy criticism
of START is embodied in the question, What are jails and
prisons for? Either it's punishment or it's rehabilitation. If it
is the former, then START did the job. But if it is rehabilitation, START failed. Punishment and behavior modification
are far from synonymous.

A number of behaviorists have struggled with the problem
of rehabilitation of prison inmates and have examined the
various programs that have failed. (START is not the only
project that has been attacked. Behavior-modification programs in prisons in Virginia and Michigan have been severely
criticized for violating individual rights of prisoners.) The big-
gest obstacle to successful rehabilitation is the prison system
itself, a system with a tradition of punishment and rigid control. A revealing example of the prevailing attitude of prison
personnel is what happened when a team of psychologists
working at the Draper Correctional Center in Elmore, Alabama, tried to teach the guards how to apply behavioral principles in their work. They hoped that this might improve the
quality of their interaction with inmates. But the psychologists
were dead wrong. The guards applied only some of the techniques they had been taught. They tended, for the most part,
to employ punishment, timeout and negative reinforcement;
positive reinforcement was rarely used. And when the psychologists asked the guards in what ways they would like to see
the prisoners improve, their responses were clear: they wanted
the prisoners to follow their orders. For the prison guards,
learning behavior-modification techniques merely gave them a
better way to control their subjects.

A second closely related impediment to successful
rehabilitation is what psychologist Kennedy calls the "powerlessness of the inmates." Except for hunger strikes and acts of

violence such as riots, prisoners have no power. This powerlessness has serious repercussions. One repercussion is physical and psychological abuse by prison personnel; because they have no means of exerting countercontrol, prisoners are defenseless targets of cruel and sadistic treatment. B. F. Skinner recognizes this problem.

> The point is illustrated by five fields in which control is not offset by countercontrol and which have therefore become classical examples of mistreatment. They are the care of the very young, of the aged, of prisoners, of psychotics, and of the retarded. It is often said that those who have these people in charge lack compassion or a sense of ethics, but the conspicuous fact is that they are not subject to strong countercontrol. The young and the aged are too weak to protest, prisoners are controlled by police power, and psychotics and retardates cannot organize or act successfully. Little or nothing is done about mistreatment unless countercontrol, usually negative, is introduced from outside.[5]

With behavioral technology added to the guards' weaponry, the inmate doesn't stand a chance.

Prisoners are aware of the lack of control they have over their fate, and the imposition of rules, points and levels only exaggerates this awareness. And people who feel powerless usually give up. Research has shown that when individuals are placed in such a situation, a number of important psychological changes occur. People tend to have less accurate perceptions of social and environmental contingencies and are less likely to remember important information that is given to them than are people who feel that they have control. One of the most important reactions is a deterioration in coping skills. People who view themselves as powerless are unlikely to initiate attempts at problem solving. Given these facts, it is not surprising that the typical prison inmate is rarely motivated to participate in rehabilitation programs, especially those that stress obedience to institutional rules and regulations.

Another problem is that the penal system doesn't allow for the gradual, step-by-step training that is one of the hallmarks of behavior modification. The ideal would be to give each inmate specific vocational and social-skill training within the institution, and then as he progressed, to continue this training in real-life (out-of-the-prison) settings. Rehabilitation is only meaningful if it involves learning the actual skills necessary to succeed on the outside. But even with a carefully supervised parole system, the transition from the prison to the real world is devastatingly abrupt. As the system now operates, the paroled prisoner is not equipped to make it. What is needed is a release program in which the prisoner could be successfully weaned from the artificial life of the institution.

It all goes back to the question, What are jails and prisons for? Given the emphasis on control, coupled with the fact that less than 10 percent of the federal budget for prisons is allocated for rehabilitation, the development of truly effective rehabilitation programs is highly unlikely. If we desire rehabilitation, there is little hope at present.

What can the behavior modifier do? Probably very little. Some behaviorists feel that the entire penal system must be revised and that those who try to set up programs within the system are doing nothing more than perpetuating a bad situation.

Remodeling the system is no easy chore and what's more, behaviorists hardly have all the answers. But some of the behaviorists' ways of analyzing human problems may offer hope. One thing that many behaviorists stress is the need for rehabilitation programs that meet the needs of the inmates rather than those of the staff. Instead of rewarding prisoners for not swearing, for instance, the emphasis should be directed toward meaningful vocational training. One of the primary goals of any prison program should be to give each inmate a readily marketable skill.

Another important reform would be to involve inmates in the running of the institution. Participation in program planning and evaluation as well as in some policy making would require that all rehabilitation programs be voluntary. Not only would this give the prisoners a real sense of control over their own lives, it would also foster the development of programs that are more relevant to the prisoners' needs.

One of the most innovative reforms that has been suggested is to differentially reward staff for the progress of the inmates. This would mean making the correctional system accountable for the success of its rehabilitation programs. If the inmate shows positive gains, staff as well as inmate would be rewarded. In his article on changing the probation system, R. L. Smith described a program in California in which communities were given funds depending on their probation success rate. The fewer the number of repeating offenders, the greater the funds. Interestingly enough it worked—offenses decreased.

We have seen, then, that behavior modification can do more harm than good when it is carelessly used within a penal system already characterized by coercion and punishment. The evidence of any improvement resulting from such programs is doubtful, while the treatment of the prisoners becomes only more dehumanizing. If behavior modification can help at all, its role would seem to be to offer new suggestions for radical system reforms, such as those we have just described.

As is clear from our discussion of the rehabilitation of criminals and from our earlier discussion of behavior modification in the schools, behavior modification can be a very effective means of one person's imposing his values on another. In the schools the techniques have been used to make children quiet and docile; in prisons, to make inmates meek and compliant. It has also been used to coerce Vietnamese mental patients to cultivate fields located in combat areas.

In 1970 Dr. Lloyd H. Cotter, a psychiatrist assigned to the Bien Hoa Mental Hospital in South Vietnam, decided to apply some of the behavior-modification techniques he had gleaned from his readings and his conversations with the staff on a behavior-modification unit at a large California mental institution. Cotter noticed the Bien Hoa patients' apathy and low interest in working; he reasoned that all they needed was proper motivation. His solution was a simple one: give the patients a choice—work or receive painful electroconvulsive shock treatments. It is important to point out that ECT (shock treatment) has in itself nothing to do with behavior modification but is a mode of temporary treatment for severe depression which produces convulsions and temporary unconsciousness by passing electrical current through the brain. It is almost always extremely unpleasant, and occasionally dangerous. What Dr. Cotter did was to use it as a form of punishment for refusing to work. Patients were asked if they wanted to go out into the fields and work. Only 10 of the 130 patients felt like working, so the next day he administered 120 shock treatments. Shock treatment was given to "nonworking" patients three times a week until all of the patients willingly agreed to go to the fields. With this success under his belt he moved on to figure out how to motivate other patients to work. His next assignment was a ward of 130 women. He used the same approach—work or ECT—but this time it was not so effective. He reported that after twenty treatments, only 15 women were working. He modified his strategy slightly and gave the women a different choice: work or no food. It took only three days and he had all 130 women out in the fields. There is no question that he had developed an effective means of behavior modification.

This program is considered by most behavior modifiers as a classic case of abuse of techniques. In the first place, Cotter failed to determine if working in the fields was the best way to therapeutically counteract the patients' apathy. Second, he did not consider the use of meaningful positive incentives. While patients did earn slightly less than one cent a day, it was clear from their refusal to work that this payment was not a sufficient reinforcer. Critics have also pointed out that the entire program may have served political motives. In his recent discussion on ethical issues in behavior modification, Professor D. A. Begelman of Kirkland College comes right to the point:

Whether the work details themselves were tailored to individual needs of his Vietnamese patients is a question which by now must strike the reader as morally insignificant in comparison to the methods utilized by Cotter. Nonetheless, he reported later in his article that the work assignments arranged for patients took the form of "ten-man agricultural teams" which were sent to garrisons in enemy territory. Presumably, the A-teams were responsible for growing crops at the garrisons, in order that the American military force deployed there be supplied with a "better diet," and the cost of the air transport of food be reduced. Apparently, these behavioral goals were established by Cotter after a casual conversation with the commander of a Special Forces group in Vietnam.[6]

Brutal punishment is not made respectable by calling it behavior modification. Such punishment seems to have been used throughout man's history to alter behavior, and it is not a new technique devised by behavioral scientists in their laboratories. Starving Vietnamese prisoners into submission could have been done (and no doubt would have been) thirty years ago, before the concepts of behavior modification had been formulated.

Skinner's observation regarding classic cases of abuse is true. An individual who, regardless of the reasons, does not have the wherewithal to exert his will, who does not have a means of countercontrol, often falls victim to cruel and unfair treatment. In the spirit of civil rights, the courts as well as various professional groups are now establishing safeguards to protect the defenseless. Although these actions are not specifically directed toward the application of behavior modification, they have direct relevance to many of the techniques used in behavioral programs.

The most important event in this movement was the 1972 *Wyatt* v. *Stickney* decision, in which the court prohibited the use of involuntary patient labor for the operation of any mental institution. The court also stated that if patients volunteer to do hospital work, they must receive the federal minimum wage.

This lawsuit was originated by a group of employees at a mental institution in Alabama who felt that planned cutbacks in personnel meant that the patients would have to assume many of the chores of operating the hospital. While the employees' concern appears to be valid, the use of patient labor has long been a common practice in most state mental hospitals; in fact, many institutions couldn't survive without it. In its defense many authorities claim that work is therapeutic. Both applied and laboratory studies have proved that idleness brings apathy and depression, but the court questioned the possibility of a conflict of interest. Does the staff assign patients the task of washing bathrooms, for instance, because it is therapeutic or because it means less work for the staff? Does the institution administration require its able-bodied patients to work on the hospital farm because hard work and sunshine are good for them or because it saves money? Mental-health lawyer Bruce Ennis has a rather novel way of determining whether or not a specific work assignment is intended to serve a therapeutic function:

> If a given type of labor *is* therapeutic, we would expect to find patients in private facilities performing that type of labor. Conversely, labor which is not generally performed in private facilities should be presumed . . . to be cost-saving rather than therapeutic.[7]

This criterion seems a little weak, however. Why wouldn't a private hospital be just as interested in saving money, if not more so, than a state facility? But regardless of exactly how the *Wyatt* decision is interpreted, it has a major effect on almost every treatment program in the country.

Behavior-modification programs are clearly affected by the fifth circuit court's decision, since most programs emphasize some kind of behavioral change. In the past, patients have been required to maintain their living quarters, participate in sheltered workshop projects and engage in work-related activities with the idea of preparing them for a life outside. Since participation is usually mandatory and reimbursement takes the form of special privileges and not salaries, these practices are in clear violation of the court's decision. But a careful reading of the *Wyatt* decision reveals the possibility of scheduling meaningful rehabilitative activities so long as they do not contribute to the maintenance and operation of the hospital.

But the real legal controversy concerning behavior modification involves a recent interpretation of the *Wyatt* decision by University of Arizona law professor David B. Wexler. He suggests that most token programs may be unconstitutional because rights guaranteed by law (i.e., the right of privacy, access to a telephone, minimum wage-standards, visitation privileges) are not freely available but rather must be earned. They are typically used as rewards for patient progress, and if a patient fails to improve, he is denied what Wexler believes to be a constitutional right. For example, in the extremely successful program for severely disturbed mental patients we discussed in chapter 8 (the Social Learning Unit in Decatur, Illinois), access to television, privacy screens for dormitories, and countless other items were used as reinforcers, which, according to Wexler's interpretation, is an unconstitutional practice. Many mental-health professionals have reacted quite strongly—claiming that the elimination of the use of such items as reinforcers in their programs would render them impotent.

Although Wexler's interpretation of the *Wyatt* decision regarding patients' constitutional rights has not been tested in court, it is being viewed by many as law. Even though Wexler himself admits in his article that the *Wyatt* decision may have to be re-evaluated, his recommendations are now being incorporated into state statutes regarding treatment of the mentally ill.

Many psychologists, behavioral and otherwise, contend that their primary ethical consideration is to achieve the maximum therapeutic benefit to the patient. It does not follow that ends justify any means, but in determining what is ethical treatment, optimum outcome for the patient must be the major consideration. But many factors must be taken into account. For this reason, mental hospitals are required to have committees composed of professionals not employed by the institution to review all treatment programs. The first issue that must be considered is, What is best for the client? The therapist's first responsibility is to serve the need of the individual who is being treated, and not some third party who may be paying for his services. According to this ethic, a psychotherapist working in a school system would be acting unethically if his first consideration was not the child's welfare but rather the needs of the teacher. He would be unethical if he designed a program to make the child quiet and docile if such behavior had no demonstrated benefit to the child.

Another important consideration is what method is the most effective and whether the procedure might involve personal pain. Pain or discomfort for the patient must be weighed against the potential benefits of the procedure. That is, what is the cost-benefit ratio of the technique? Given two equally effective methods, the therapist would choose the least intrusive (e.g., positive reinforcement over punishment). But by the same token the therapist would not refuse to use punishment if it was the only effective method—though he would always use the least painful method available. Dr. Lovaas' work with self-destructive children, which we discussed in chapter 8, is a prime example. Given his treatment alternatives (i.e., permanent heavy sedation and the physical restraints of a strait jacket), the punishment procedure was clearly the best and most ethical. In fact, it would have been unethical not to use the procedure. But by the same line of reasoning, Cotter's program for the Vietnamese mental patients was clearly unethical. First, it seems highly likely that nonaversive techniques would have been equally effective. (From Cotter's report it appears that he did not even check to find out if a positive-reinforcement system would have worked). Second, it is quite possible that the massive exposure to shock treatment might have caused serious injury. And finally, the goals of Cotter's program were not in the patients' best interests. It is clear from this comparison of two instances in which punishment has been used in behavioral programs that the morality of a treatment program is not solely determined by the particular techniques that are used but rather by the circumstances in which the program is carried out. Because of the enormous complexity of the issues involved in psychotherapy, it is naïve to think that a simple set of rules will follow from legal debate.

But even with the implementation of elaborate safeguards and review committees, many people fear the power that behavior modification gives its user. Former North Carolina Senator Sam J. Ervin, Jr., expresses this concern in his preface to a report on the federal government's role in behavior modification:

> To my mind the most serious threat posed by the technology of behavior modification is the power this technology gives one man to impose his values on another. . . . If our society is to remain free, one man must not be empowered to change another man's personality.[8]

The fear is that behavior modification can be used against a person's will. Unfortunately this fear is, at least in part, justified.

The kind of aversive conditioning described in *A Clockwork Orange* would not be the way to bring about ultimate control. A number of research studies have shown that aversive-conditioning procedures are not effective if the subject is not motivated to change. In his recent book on aversion therapy in prisons, Stanley J. Dirks reported that in cases when inmates were coerced, the treatment did not result in changed behavior. And in both laboratory and hospital research with alcoholics and homosexuals, conditioning therapies failed to alter permanently the behavior of unwilling patients. The only aspect of Burgess's book that was truly science fiction was that the aversive techniques he described actually "cured" Alex's "problem."

But there are other techniques. A way that behavior

modification might be used on us without our knowledge or resistance would be in the form of positive-reinforcement systems. A sophisticated would-be controller would, quite simply, use honey instead of vinegar. He would devise elaborate ways to reward us each time we made any signs of adopting his values. It would be subtle and difficult to resist. And as the theory predicts, our behavior would be slowly modified.

This is the strategy the Chinese Communists used to brainwash American soldiers imprisoned during the Korean War. Prisoners were not tortured, drugged or subjected to psychic surgery, as many leading psychiatrists and psychologists of the day presumed. Rather, they were generously, though unobtrusively rewarded for any expression of anti-Americanism. The program had two aims—first, to prevent any attempt by the prisoners to escape or band together to fight the indoctrination, and second, to develop anti-American and anticapitalistic philosophies among the soldiers.

Prisoners were housed in modest, though comfortable quarters and were given good food and plenty of exercise. The situation resembled a school rather than a prison, and in fact, the captured soldiers were never called prisoners—they were "students." In addition to attending daily lectures on Communist doctrine, they also participated in group discussions. In these sessions the men were asked to talk about their experiences and thoughts. If they were cooperative, they received extra cigarettes, candy and money, as well as the praise of their teachers. The system moved slowly—with prisoners being gradually encouraged to criticize the actions of their fellow Americans in the camp. The effect was to erode the group's solidarity and cohesiveness, until finally the men did not trust one another. Thus, rebellion was quashed before it ever started, and the men did not even know it.

Anti-American feelings were shaped. At first any hints of such sentiments earned extra privileges and cigarettes. For example, in art recreation periods, certain themes were reinforced. A picture of Harry Truman with bloody claws earned a monetary prize, whereas a painting of a beautiful woman was not considered art. The men were also rewarded for writing articles for American newspapers against the U.S. campaign. Within eight to twelve months of such "education" and behavior modification, the men began taking an active role in the Communist propaganda activities.

Psychologists Donald Whaley and Richard Malott offer a fascinating analysis of the brainwashing program in their book *Elementary Principles of Behavior:*

> The types of things which had been done to them seemed simple, almost humane, and had not appeared to be directed toward "breaking" them or reducing them to the form of lower animals. Upon analysis, it was found that the techniques were basic and simple principles of operant [behavioral] psychology. Almost all of the important behavior changes were brought about by the use of reinforcement in the form of cigarettes, sweets, or privileges. . . .
>
> . . . It was quite obvious that the behavioral changes had been brought about so gradually and in such a subtle manner that many of our troops were not aware that they had changed appreciably or that what they were doing was in any way disloyal or anti-American.[9]

The reason that any would-be controller would choose reinforcement over punishment is apparent from the preceding example. There is less chance of the citizenry resisting. People would be more likely to fight back if force were used. Skinner points out that many state governments have become aware of the advantages of positive control:

> The fact that positive reinforcement does not breed countercontrol has not gone unnoticed by would-be controllers, who have simply shifted to positive means. Here is an example: A government must raise money. If it does so through taxation, its citizens must pay or be punished, and they may escape from this aversive control by putting another party in power at the next election. As an alternative, the government organizes a

lottery, and instead of being forced to pay taxes, the citizens *voluntarily* buy tickets. The result is the same: the citizens give the government money, but they feel free and do not protest in the second case. Nevertheless they are being controlled, as powerfully as by a threat of punishment, by that particularly powerful (variable-ratio) schedule of reinforcement.[10]

Skinner was appalled when he learned of Illinois' Instant Lottery, in which players are buying the opportunity to be reinforced immediately. The player buys a ticket, wets the back side and knows right away whether or not he got the lucky ticket. It is a lot more enticing than the regular weekly or monthly lotteries. In southern Illinois, ticket sales jumped 1,000 percent when the system switched from weekly to immediate payoffs.

How do we protect ourselves against abuse of behavioral technology? We cannot outlaw behavior modification; it pervades everything we do. And as the previous chapters attest, it provides the most effective form of therapy for many individuals. Review boards, institutional guidelines and public disclosure, as well as rigorous training of teachers and mental-health personnel, are all important methods of protection. But the most important safeguards are public awareness and effective means of countercontrol. We must understand what is being done to us in order to exert our own control. And steps in this direction are being taken. Recently Ralph Nader's group published a consumer's guide to psychotherapy. Beth Israel Hospital in Boston gives each patient a pamphlet entitled "Your Right as a Patient," which lets the patient know what to expect and what he can do if he believes he is getting inadequate care. As we mentioned earlier, one of the functions of this book is to serve as a consumer's guide to behavior modification. Regardless of the product, the educated consumer is at an advantage. In the case of this particular product, education is not only an advantage, but a necessity.

XI

Nonbehavioral Behavior Modification

Throughout this book we have stressed the point that behavior modification represents a fundamental departure from traditional methods of psychotherapy. The behavior modifier attempts to alleviate psychological problems not by changing people's psyches but by changing their behavior.

However, we must point out that many avowed behaviorists are broadening their view of human behavior and its causes. These nonradical behaviorists realize that human actions, more than just overt responses to stimuli and events in the environment, are also affected by thoughts and emotions. Of course behaviorists have always acknowledged the existence of mental processes, but until recently they have downplayed their importance in determining our actions. As we discussed earlier in the book, B. F. Skinner considers such things as mere by-products of reinforcement and punishment, but not all behaviorists agree with Skinner. They are now extending their domain to include thinking, or what they call *covert behavior*.

This "broadened" approach to behavior modification does not mean that behaviorists are either adopting Freudian notions of hidden conflicts within the psyche or turning to techniques such as free association and dream analysis. Nor does it mean that they are denying the importance of reinforcement and punishment. What it does mean is that a new element has been added to the behaviorists' list of factors that influence our behavior. Former president of the American Psychological Association and a leader in the Behavior Modification movement, Albert Bandura, states the assumptions of what we have labeled "nonradical behaviorism":

> Human functioning, in fact, involves interrelated control systems in which behavior is determined by external stimulus events, by internal information—processing systems and regulatory codes, and by reinforcing response-feedback processes.[1]

Perhaps without realizing it, radical behaviorists have also recognized the importance of thinking and emotions in their work. They ask their clients to introspect and examine feelings, to imagine traumatic situations and to take conscious control of their own behavior. When one carefully studies the behaviorist's methods, Professor Edwin Locke's question seems quite appropriate: "Is 'Behavior Therapy' Behavioristic?" It appears that many of the techniques contradict at least some of the basic tenets of behavioral psychology. One thing is clear: the charge that behavior modification is mindless psychology is inaccurate.

This nonradical approach to behavior modification has received at least three names: "Cognitive Behavior Modification," "Rational Restructuring" and "Attribution Therapy." Essentially it involves modifying behavior by influencing the individual's ways of conceptualizing the world, or at least certain aspects of his world. The main focus of this approach has been to teach people to adopt more rational interpretations of events in their lives and to give them more effective problem-solving strategies.

People often overreact to situations. Depending on how we interpret it, a casual remark or insignificant act can affect our emotions and subsequent behavior. Consider a situation in which an acquaintance passes by but does not speak. Paul is reading his newspaper as he rides the commuter train home at 5:30. The train stops and a friend gets on and takes the empty seat across the aisle. Paul continues to read his newspapers but starts to wonder why he was snubbed. He is mildly annoyed, feels a little rejected, but says nothing. A few minutes later he goes to the club car for a drink. He does not ask his friend to join him. But Paul's reaction might have been quite different if he'd interpreted his friend's behavior differently. Perhaps his friend was just preoccupied and really didn't notice him or perhaps the friend saw that he was reading and didn't want to disturb him. If Paul had adopted either of the latter interpretations he would not have reacted negatively; in fact, he might have appreciated his friend's consideration and asked him to join him in the club car. Admittedly, this example is simple, but it does demonstrate the point. How we react to a situation and the effect it has on our behavior is as much dependent on our interpretation of the situation as it is on the situation itself.

Why do people misinterpret situations? One of the most common reasons, according to many psychologists, is that people often approach a new situation with preconceived assumptions about its outcome—what is known as a "set." Take the optimist and the pessimist. Each would react differently to the situation of taking a test for a new job. The optimist would be eager and confident and begin to work as soon as he gets the test materials. The pessimist, we need hardly explain, would be considerably more anxious and less eager to try because he is already convinced that he is not going to do well. Not surprisingly, research has shown that the set that people adopt has a very significant effect on their performance.

When a nonradical behavior modifier has a client who appears to react to new situations in self-defeating ways he tries to change his client's set. By changing the way the client interprets things, the therapist hopes to eliminate his maladaptive behaviors.

Sometimes people's misinterpretations are related to their ignorance of the real causes of a particular situation or event. An especially dramatic case was reported by psychologist Gerald C. Davison. The client was a forty-year-old truckdriver admitted to a Veterans Administration hospital because he believed he was crazy. He reported that a "spirit" was communicating with him by applying pressure to a spot over his right eye. The disturbance appeared to have begun shortly after his brother's suicide, when the client started having painful muscle spasms over the heart and the right eye, and in the abdomen. Dr. Davison interviewed the patient and reasoned that the twitches were anxiety reactions in the form of severe muscle tension. To test out his hypothesis he asked the patient to clench his fist to create extreme muscle tension. The patient agreed that this sensation was the same as what he believed the spirit was causing. Dr. Davison then explained his theory to the patient—perhaps the pressure and tension are not caused by spirits at all but are, in fact, natural reactions to being very tense in certain situations. During the next sessions the patient received progressive relaxation training and learned to reduce tension by tightening and then releasing various muscle groups. Dr. Davison then instructed him to do these exercises whenever he felt the sensation of pressure. In order to convince the patient that his symptoms were, in fact, a natural reaction to anxiety-provoking situations, Dr. Davison set up a situation that he felt would evoke anxiety in the patient—a game of blackjack. As they played, the patient did experience the tension, and when it became acute, Dr. Davison suggested that he begin the relaxation exercises he had been taught. As he started tightening and releasing his muscles the tension disappeared. The patient was able to follow Dr. Davison's instructions and successfully eliminate the spasms. After a month of doing the exercises whenever he felt pressure building up, he began to abandon the idea that he was receiving communications from a spirit.

During the last weeks of hospitalization the patient learned to identify situations that might cause his anxiety and what he might do to change those situations. Dr. Davison also discussed the importance of the patient's learning to assert his wishes in appropriate ways so as to avoid interpersonal conflict and the emotional outbursts that seemed to make him anxious. A follow-up six weeks after the patient's release from the hospital revealed continued improvement. He reported that he felt the tension less frequently and that he could control it by his relaxation exercises. Other aspects of his life, such as his marriage and work, also showed improvement.

Impotence is another problem where the individual's interpretation of an event may evoke maladaptive emotional reactions. Many men become panicky when they are unable, for one reason or another, to maintain an erection. They fear that they have lost their masculinity, have some deep-seated neurosis or are getting old. This interpretation leads to a great deal of anxiety. At the next opportunity for intercourse they are eager to perform and disprove their fears. But because they are anxious, they are impotent again. A vicious cycle develops, so that the fear of being impotent makes them impotent. This in turn often leads to depression and other problems. As Masters and Johnson have pointed out, sometimes a little education would be all the man needed. If our impotent male had better understood the physiology of sexual behavior, his misinterpretation of his initial impotence might have been avoided along with the anxiety. Perhaps the reason he was impotent was that he had had too much to drink, was overly tired or had had a bad day at the office—all more likely causes than the anxiety-provoking ones he had generated. Masters and Johnson have found that the problem we describe is very common. After one incident of being impotent, many older men figure it's "all over" and more or less give up. This is especially tragic, since sexual prowess does not necessary diminish with age.

Unfortunately, many men do not have the opportunity to receive treatment from such competent practitioners as Masters and Johnson. The person troubled by impotence often seeks the help of a physician who knows very little about sexual functioning and is only able to offer his sympathy: "Sorry, bud, you'll just have to live with it."

We could give other examples of how a person's interpretation of things gets him into trouble, but we will now turn to the work of three people who are primarily interested in problems that involve people's misinterpreting events in their lives.

The foremost authority in this area is psychologist Albert Ellis. He contends that many people overreact to events and interactions because they hold a set of irrational beliefs about the way the world should be. And because things rarely match up to these rigid standards, the person views himself and his life as failures. One of the most common irrational beliefs is that one should be loved and respected by everyone. When this is one of the person's primary goals in life, he is overly sensitive to people's reactions and is therefore often disappointed and frustrated in his interactions with others. Another self-defeating belief is that one should be competent in everything he does. Again, since individuals rarely succeed at everything they do, this belief leads to a lot of misery. The person interprets everything that happens to him in terms of whether or not it meets his unrealistic standards. Rather than discarding or in some way altering his maladaptive belief system, such a person becomes upset and depressed because his life fails to meet his demanding expectations.

The goal of therapy is to persuade the individual to abandon his irrational belief system so that he can respond to events more adaptively. Ellis begins therapy by identifying the actual situations and events that cause the patient to become upset and then determines the person's underlying belief system. Although Ellis recognizes that individuals differ in the particular beliefs they hold, he has discovered certain irrational and self-defeating beliefs that are common in our culture:

1. The belief that one should be loved by everyone for everything one does—as opposed to the more realistic notion that

each person is unique and that one can be a worthwhile individual even if only certain people recognize one's assets.

2. The idea that one should be thoroughly competent in all aspects of life—as opposed to the realization that everyone has limitations.

3. The notion that it is catastrophic when things are not exactly the way one might want them to be—instead of striving to improve situations rather than agonizing over their imperfections.

4. The belief that one is virtually powerless to determine whether or not one experiences personal happiness or misery —instead of the realization that one's emotional reactions are caused as much by the interpretation one makes as they are by the events themselves.

5. The notion that certain people are evil and wicked and should be severely punished for their acts—as opposed to the notion that when people do inflict pain or suffering on others, steps can and should be taken to help them change.

6. The belief that it is better to avoid life's difficulties rather than face them—instead of the realization that one cannot avoid certain unpleasantness and that, in the long run, it is often better to resolve problems than to avoid them.

7. The idea that one's past history plays an all-important role in determining one's present condition and that one cannot overcome those effects—as opposed to the idea that one can exert some control over one's life.

Like many behaviorists, Ellis does not focus on the client's early childhood experiences, nor is he interested in developing elaborate hypotheses as to why the person has adopted such a rigid belief system. Ellis focuses on the "here and now." His approach is direct: determine the irrational aspects of the client's belief system, point out the absurdity of those beliefs and get the client to adopt a more rational perspective on his life.

Other authorities have similar theories regarding the factors that contribute to self-defeating emotional reactions. Psychiatrist Aaron Beck of the University of Pennsylvania Medical School has identified four patterns of maladaptive thinking. The first is the tendency to draw erroneous conclusions from insufficient information. It's the common problem of "reading things into" what people say and do (like our example of a person's reaction to someone's failing to say hello when they meet). Beck refers to these tendencies as arbitrary inference. Another problem is what he calls overgeneralization. The person decides after one experience that things will never change. Usually this occurs in terms of failure experience—the person who is awkward in his first sexual encounter believes that he'll always fail and therefore should not try again. The third irrational thought process, magnification, involves the person's exaggerating the meaning of an event. Beck gives the example of a hypochrondriac who thinks that every pain in his body is a sign of some fatal disease. The fourth self-defeating pattern of thinking is dichotomous reasoning. It refers to people's attending to the negative aspects of a situation and ignoring the positive (e.g., if something is not perfect, then it's worthless). While all of these maladaptive patterns might not be found within a single individual, each has the effect of reducing the likelihood of the person's engaging in activities that bring personal satisfaction and reinforcement.

These notions are further developed by psychologist Arnold Lazarus, who states that many people tend to evaluate things in black/white, right/wrong terms, with the tendency to view something as negative if it is not totally positive. Since things are rarely so clear-cut, the individual usually concludes that he is a failure and that his life is unsatisfying. Lazarus also emphasizes that the acceptance of social mores as truths cause difficulty for people. Ellis, Beck and Lazarus point out that many people make themselves miserable by viewing the world in terms of a set of illogical and rigid standards.

As with most methods of psychotherapy, the therapist begins by making a detailed assessment of the client's situation. If the major problem involves the ways the client interprets the world around him, then the therapist might, after explaining the rationale of the therapy, describe the kinds of irrational thoughts held by many people. The goal is not to have the client pinpoint which unrealistic beliefs he holds, but rather to have him think about how he might be misinterpreting events in his life. In order to demonstrate to the client the irrational nature of his attitudes, the therapist often asks him to carry those beliefs to their "logical" conclusion.

The client is also given homework assignments that require him to apply his newly acquired ways of viewing things in situations that usually make him upset.

The following passage is taken from a group therapy session in which a therapist is working with students who display great anxiety when faced with college examinations.

> *Therapist:* If you enter a situation with the attitude that "I must be perfect on this test," you will be anxious, because you can't be perfect. You set yourself up for failure right away. "I must do well on my exam, otherwise there are going to be people that will disapprove of me. They will not love me, therefore I will be no good." Yes, it would be nice—it would be very nice—if people would like you. It would be nice if you could do very well in all kinds of things. But there is a difference between "it would be nice" and "must." I think that the problem you may be experiencing when it comes to taking tests, and perhaps other situations as well, is that you may be overly harsh in what you demand of yourself. There is no reason why you cannot evaluate situations logically and intellectually from a more sensible point of view. You can say to yourself: "First of all, the chances are that if I do poorly on this test, people are still going to like me. Second of all, even if they don't like me, what kind of people are not going to like me just because I don't do well on a test? Are these friends? Are these people that are important to me?" So you can analyze the situation in terms of the chances of your worst fears coming to pass. And, if they actually did, would it really be so terrible?
>
> *Client #4:* My husband would like me to be perfect in everything that I do. But interestingly enough, he himself

doesn't strive for that. When I take tests, I think I try to prove to him that I can do really well.

Therapist: What would happen if you didn't do really well? Would he think less of you as a person?

Client #4: No, I think the problem is within myself.

Therapist: What would he think of you if you didn't do well? Would he ask for a divorce?

Client #4: No.

Therapist: Would he say "You have to pack up your bags and leave because you didn't do well on that test"?

Client #4: No, obviously not.

Client #1: It sounds almost as if it's a parent-child relationship.

Therapist: There is a remnant of childlike thinking if you must be perfect, otherwise you're nothing. You must be loved, otherwise you're hated.[2]

While these methods may have great intuitive appeal, there are skeptics who argue that techniques used to "restructure" the way people interpret things involve a lot more than getting the client to realize the irrationality of his thinking. For one thing, the client is often verbally punished by the therapist for expressing illogical thoughts, and at the same time, heavily reinforced for changing his statements. The therapist also tries to impose a specific value system on the client. The main premise is that one should accept oneself as good and valuable, regardless of one's objective capabilities. But what is the therapist going to do with someone who really is a failure and whose negative perceptions are not totally inaccurate? With such an individual, skill training would also be necessary. In his critique of these "cognitive" approaches, psychologist Michael J. Mahoney of the Pennsylvania State University points out that the claim that more positive and less self-defeating ways of viewing the world are more rational is not necessarily true. That is, "There is nothing inherently more logical about personal happiness—it just feels better."[3]

But many of us might view the critics' quarrels as just

academic. After all, their effectiveness is what counts. True. But although there are a large number of case studies in which these methods have produced positive changes, they have not been subjected to rigorous scientific examination, so it is not yet clear why these techniques work as well as they do.

Another technique that is sometimes considered non-behavioral is teaching people effective problem-solving skills. These involve considering all available solutions to a problem before acting. While this may seem to be just plain common sense, many individuals fail to use these skills adequately. Research has shown that impulsive children and adolescents as well as disturbed adults are deficient in such skills, and thus are unable to cope with a variety of real-life situations. For many of these individuals the problem appears to be an inability to generate viable solutions. Their means of handling problems often involves aggression rather than reason.

To teach more effective problem-solving strategies, the behavior therapist begins by directing the individual through each stage of the process: he defines the problem, generates possible solutions, verifies the utility of each, and then selects the best alternative. For children, training often begins by the therapist or teacher making up stories and having the children decide what the person in the story should do to solve his problem. The children are then asked to think of situations where they have had a problem and what they might have done to solve it. Role playing is also used so that the person can try out new methods of dealing with real-life difficulties. Although research in the area is scant, there is evidence that training in problem solving can have beneficial effects. Psychologists George Spivak and Myrna B. Shure have conducted a rather detailed study of the effects of such training with young children. They report that children who learn to think through problem situations before acting are less likely to be impatient and display aggressive and dominating behaviors. They also found that children were less disruptive and showed greater academic progress in regular classrooms following specific training in problem solving. And both delinquent adolescents and their parents benefit from such programs.

Another important application of problem-solving training is in crisis intervention. In emotionally stressful situations like divorce or the death of a loved one, the primary role of a therapist or counselor may be to help the person decide what to do. The goal in this case is not to teach new problem-solving strategies, but rather to assist the person to use the skills he already possesses in thinking through his situation and making rational decisions. Such counseling usually involves having the distressed individual go through each of the steps of problem solving. The client might be asked to verbalize each problem and the possible solutions. Even if some of the person's problems do not have real solutions, a systematic approach dealing with the crisis can help the individual gain a clearer perspective of his situation.

To many, the notion of nonbehavioral behavior modification may seem to be contradictory, and in a sense it is. But remember that behaviorists are pragmatic and empirical. Given obvious moral restrictions, if a behavior modifier finds a technique that produces an observable positive effect, he is likely to use it.

XII
Who's in Control?

While behavioral methods themselves may be value-free, the people who use them are not. According to their own theory, behavior modifiers are influenced by the society in which they live. The things they do, both as professionals and as private citizens, reflect the values of society. But by the same token, the behavior-modification movement has had a powerful, though subtle impact on societal values. The notion that contingencies of reward and punishment play a major role in determining our actions has been gradually integrated into our legal, social and educational systems. This phenomenon is clearly reciprocal.

The practices of behavior modifiers, and the standards that are used to evaluate them, have radically changed during the last fifteen years. Even the critics who argued during the 1960's that behavioral methods for treating severely disturbed schizophrenic patients were superficial and would surely lead to the development of even more serious disorders never suggested that the methods might violate human rights. But with the increasing concern for the rights of the individual, behavior modifiers have begun to view some of their practices from a different perspective. And to their astonishment, many of their programs appeared to have served the status quo more than the people they treated. In a great number of cases, therapy made the disturbed person docile and better able to fit into the easy operation of the institution, rather than prepared for a productive life in society. Although this "hidden" purpose of "rehabilitation" programs did not originate with behavior modification, many of the early programs did serve it.

Behavior modifiers also question the extent to which their offering treatment for the elimination of certain behaviors defines the behavior as a problem. The most controversial example of this issue is the treatment of homosexuals. Gay Liberation spokesmen, as well as the former president of the Association for the Advancement of Behavior Therapy, Gerald Davison, object to the very existence of such treatment programs because they legitimize society's stigmatization of homosexuals. Since the American Psychiatric Association removed homosexuality, in 1973, from the list of mental disorders in its diagnostic manual, many argue that therapy designed to change a person's sexual orientation is wrong. Rather, psychotherapists should help the person resolve the anxiety and guilt that might be associated with his homosexuality, while directing their efforts toward changing society's derogation of diverse life styles. Though not all psychotherapists who call themselves behaviorists share Davison's opinion, there is a growing concern regarding the de facto disparagement associated with certain treatment programs. In fact, behavior modifiers have been more active than any other group or mental-health professionals in recognizing the ethical issues in psychotherapy.

With this raised consciousness among professionals, there is also the realization that in many ways the behavior-modification movement has done much to increase the dignity of the individual seeking help. The behavior therapist asks the client to specify the goals of therapy. The therapist is not placed in the role of an all-knowing authority who tells the client what his "real," underlying problem is. The behavior therapist takes the role more of a consultant whose purpose it is to assist the person in changing those aspects of his life that he finds unfulfilling or painful. Another positive aspect of behavior modification is the awareness of the individual's uniqueness. There are no set packages or psychological "prescriptions." Behavioral programs are individualized.

The impact that behavior modification has had on societal values is not insignificant. There is considerable controversy regarding the implications that behavioral psychology has for our legal system. If the environment plays a significant role in determining people's actions, then to what extent can an individual be held accountable for his misdoings? The Patty Hearst case is a prime example. The defense argued that she was coerced into committing bank robbery. They claimed she was not responsible; the blame lies with the environmental contingencies imposed by the Symbionese Liberation Army. The argument involves not the plea of temporary insanity, but environmental control.

Behavior theory also affects our welfare and education policies. Agencies are becoming increasingly aware of some of the undesirable side effects of certain reinforcement contingencies that are implicit in our social system. With this awareness of the environment's powerful effect, new strategies are being introduced to better help and educate disadvantaged individuals.

The accomplishments of behavioral psychology, and behavior modification in particular, have implications which challenge our notions regarding the nature of man and society. Behavior theory is inconsistent with many of our basic beliefs. How do we deal with the legal concepts of personal responsibility, guilt and innocence? What is coercion? Is the heroin addict coerced into stealing by the need to supply his habit and avoid painful withdrawal symptoms? Is the middle-class salesman coerced into white-collar crime by the pressure to feed his family and keep up with the Joneses? And is the academically unsuccessful sixteen-year-old male coerced into vandalism by the desire to be accepted by his peers? Is the individual who engages in antisocial behavior a criminal or the victim of an unfortunate set of environmental contingencies?

Are we really the masters of our own minds? How, indeed, do we reconcile the concept of environmental control with free will?

Source Notes

Chapter I

1. Kittrie, N., "The Promised Land of Behavior Control," Washington *Post* (March 12, 1972).

Chapter III

1. Eysenck, H. J., *The Causes and Cures of Neurosis* (San Diego, Calif.: Robert R. Knapp, 1965), p. 268
2. Stuart, R. B., *Trick or Treatment: How and When Psychotherapy Fails* (Champaign, Ill.: Research Press, 1970), p. 58.
3. Fenichel, O., *The Psychoanalytic Theory of Neurosis* (London: Routledge and Kegan Paul, 1946), pp. 232–233.

Chapter V

1. Stunkard, A. J., "New Treatments for Obesity: Behavior Modification," in G. A. Bray and J. E. Bethune, ed., *Treatment and Management of Obesity* (New York: Harper & Row, 1974), p. 103.

Chapter VI

1. Paul, G. L., "Outcome of Systematic Desensitization," in C. M. Franks, ed., *Behavior Therapy: Appraisal and Outcome* (New York: McGraw-Hill, 1969), p. 159.
2. O'Leary, K. D., and Wilson, G. T., *Behavior Therapy Application and Outcome* (Englewood Cliffs, N.J.: Prentice-Hall, 1975), p. 289.

Chapter VIII

1. Greenfeld, J., *A Child Called Noah* (New York: Warner Books, 1970), pp. 12–14.
2. Zax, M., and Stricker, G., *Patterns of Psychopathology* (New York: Macmillan, 1963), pp. 64–66.
3. Lovaas, O. I., Koegel, R., Simmons, J. Q., and Long, J. S., "Some Generalization and Follow-up Measures on Autistic Children in Behavior Therapy," *Journal of Applied Behavioral Analysis* (1973), *6*, p. 163.
4. *Ibid.*, p. 157.
5. *Ibid.*, p. 160.
6. Paul, G. L., and Lentz, J., *Psychosocial Treatment of Chronically Institutionalized Mental Patients: A Comparative Study of Milieu versus Social Learning Programs* (in process).

Chapter IX

1. Becker, W. C., Madsen, C. H., Arnold, C. R., and Thomas, D. R., "The Contingent Use of Teacher Attention and Praise in Reducing Classroom Behavior Problems," *Journal of Special Education* (1967), *1*, p. 292.
2. *Ibid.*, p. 294.
3. *Ibid.*, p. 294–296.
4. *Ibid.*, p. 296.
5. Winett, R. A., and Winkler, R. C., "Current Behavior Modification in the Classroom: Be Still, Be Quiet, Be Docile," *Journal of Applied Behavior Analysis* (1972), *5*, p. 500.
6. *Ibid.*, p. 500.

Chapter X

1. Mitford, J., "The Torture Cure: Winning Criminal Hearts and Minds with Drugs, Scalpels, and Sensory Deprivation," *Harper's* (August 1973), p. 26.
2. From a letter written to Dr. Pasquale J. Ciccone by Arpiar G. Saunders, Jr., February 16, 1973.
3. Cohen, H. L., "The Person: To Be or Not to Be," address given to the Association for the Advancement of Behavior Therapy, Chicago, Ill., 1974, p. 4 (unpublished).
4. McConnell, J. V., "Criminals Can Be Brainwashed—Now," *Psychology Today* (1970), *3*, p. 74.
5. Skinner, B. F., *About Behaviorism* (New York: Knopf, 1974), p. 191.
6. Begelman, D. A., "Ethical and Legal Issues in Behavior Modification," in M. Hersen, R. M. Eisler and P. M. Miller, ed., *Progress in Behavior Modification*, Vol. I (New York: Academic Press, 1975), pp. 167–168.
7. Wexler, D. B., "Token and Taboo: Behavior Modification, Token Economies, and the Law," *Behaviorism* (1973), *1*, p. 11.
8. Ervin, S. J., *Individual Rights and the Federal Role in Behavior Modification* (Washington, D.C.: U.S. Government Printing Office, 1974), p. iii.
9. Whaley, D. L., and Malott, R. W., *Elementary Principles of Behavior* (Englewood Cliffs, N.J.: Prentice-Hall, 1971), pp. 220–221.
10. Skinner, B. F., *About Behaviorism* (New York: Knopf, 1974), p. 198.

Chapter XI

1. Bandura, A., *Principles of Behavior Modification* (New York: Holt, Rinehart & Winston, 1969), p. 19.
2. Goldfried, M. R., and Goldfried, A. P., "Cognitive Change Methods," in F. H. Kanfer and A. P. Goldstein, ed., *Helping People Change* (New York: Pergamon Press, 1975), pp. 97–98.
3. Mahoney, M. J., *Cognition and Behavior Modification* (Cambridge, Mass.: Ballinger, 1974), p. 184.

Index

About the Authors

WILLIAM H. REDD received his Ph.D. in psychology at the University of North Carolina at Chapel Hill and is now Associate Professor of Psychology at the University of Illinois at Urbana-Champaign. Before joining the faculty at Illinois, he worked as a clinician and researcher at the Fernald School and the Massachusetts General Hospital in Boston. During that period he also held teaching appointments at Harvard and at Boston University.

Dr. Redd is a fellow of the Behavior Therapy and Research Society, and is a member of the American Psychological Association and the Society for Research in Child Development.

WILLIAM SLEATOR is the author of five books: *The Angry Moon* (1970), *Blackbriar* (1972), *Run* (1973), *House of Stairs* (1974)—a young-adult novel based on behavior modification—and *Among the Dolls* (1975.) A 1967 graduate of Harvard College, he was also a Fellow at the Bread Loaf Writers' Conference in 1969. A resident of Boston, he is the company pianist for the Boston Ballet Company and the composer of a ballet recently performed by that company.

DATE DUE
